Deconstruction II

BERNARD TSCHUMI, NEW NATIONAL THEATRE OF JAPAN, TOKYO, PERSPECTIVE

BEHNISCH & PARTNERS, HYSOLAR INSTITUTE, UNIVERSITY OF STUTTGART, EXTERIOR DETAIL

An Architectural Design Profile

Deconstruction II

ARQUITECTONICA, MIRACLE PLACE, MIAMI, RENDERING

ACADEMY EDITIONS LONDON

Acknowledgements

Front Cover: Daniel Libeskind, Berlin 'City Edge', Alpha Model, photo by Hélène Binet; *Back Cover*: Peter Eisenman, Museum of the 21st Century, Rovereto, photo by Dick Frank; *Inside Front Cover*: Peter Wilson, Amsterdam Bridge, screenprint; *Inside Back Cover*: Morphosis, Kate Mantilini Restaurant, Santa Monica, photo by Tom Bonner; *Half Title Page*: Bernard Tschumi, New National Theatre of Japan, Tokyo, perspective view of lobby; *Frontis*: Günter Behnisch & Partners, Hysolar Institute, University of Stuttgart, exterior detail, photo by Christian Kandzia; *Title Page*: Arquitectonica, Miracle Place, Miami, rendering; *Contents Page*: Hiromi Fujii, Mizoe-2, Fukuoka, view from east, photo by Shigeo Ogawa/Shinkenchiku, courtesy of the architect.

Jacques Derrida
pp6-11: This discussion is an edited transcript of a video interview with Derrida recorded in the context of the International Symposium on Deconstruction at the Tate Gallery in March 1988. An expanded presentation with additional material will appear in the forthcoming *Deconstruction Omnibus Volume* (Academy Editions). Photograph James Friedman, courtesy of Peter Eisenman.

Bernard Tschumi
pp12-19: All material supplied by the architect.

Daniel Libeskind
pp20-39: All material supplied by the architect. Photographs for the Berlin 'City Edge' projects are: 'Cloud Prop' models by Hélène Binet and Uwe Rau; Villa on Lutzowplatz by Uwe Rau; the Alef Wing by Dino Scrimali and Leo Torri; 'Never is the Center' by Dino Scrimali. Line of Fire by Hélène Binet, this was exhibited as an installation at the Centre d'Art Contemporain de Geneve in 1988.

Peter Eisenman
pp40-62: All material supplied by the architect. Photographs by Dick Frank.

Andrew Benjamin
pp63-66: This article also appears in the *Oxford Art Journal*, April 1989. Illustration courtesy of Peter Eisenman.

Hiromi Fujii
pp67-75: English translation by Hiroshi Watanabe. Illustrations supplied by the author.

Stanley Tigerman
pp76-81: This text forms the draft introduction to the author's forthcoming book, *Failed Attempts at Healing an Irreparable Wound*. Illustrative material supplied by the author.

Günter Behnisch & Partners
pp82-87: All material supplied by Günter Behnisch. Photographs by Christian Kandzia.

Morphosis
pp 88-96: Texts and graphic material supplied by the architects. Photographs of Kate Mantilini Restaurant by Tom Bonner and Tim Street-Porter and of the Comprehensive Cancer Center by Tom Bonner.

Editor: Dr Andreas C Papadakis

First published in Great Britain in 1989
New edition published in Great Britain in 1994 by *Architectural Design*
an imprint of the
ACADEMY GROUP LTD, 42 LEINSTER GARDENS, LONDON W2 3AN
MEMBER OF THE VCH PUBLISHING GROUP
ISBN: 1 85490 242 3

Architectural Design Profile 77 is published as part of *Architectural Design* Vol 59 1/2 1989
Architectural Design Magazine is published six times a year and is available by subscription

Distributed in the United States of America by
ST MARTIN'S PRESS, 175 FIFTH AVENUE, NEW YORK, NY 10010

Printed and bound in Singapore

Contents

HIROMI FUJII, MIZOE-2, FUKUOKA, JAPAN, VIEW FROM EAST

PETER EISENMAN, WEXNER CENTER FOR THE VISUAL ARTS, OHIO STATE UNIVERSITY

JACQUES DERRIDA
In Discussion with Christopher Norris

Of circumstantial detail it is perhaps enough to record that this interview was conducted at Derrida's home near Paris during a two-hour session in March, 1988. He had wanted to attend the Tate Symposium and participate in a panel discussion with Bernard Tschumi, Peter Eisenman, Charles Jencks and others. In the event he was unable to make the trip and instead arranged with Symposium organiser Andreas Papadakis to do a video interview, screened as part of the Symposium proceedings. There was no time to submit questions or do much in the way of advance planning, but as it turned out this was no problem: the interview covered all the main points I had hoped to raise, along with various related topics. Derrida kindly agreed to speak in English, which helped a great deal when it came to the screening and subsequent audience discussion. In editing the transcript I have slightly expanded some of my questions to improve continuity and to offer some signposts or contextual cues for readers unfamiliar with Derrida's work. I have taken this opportunity to reconstruct one or two passages where the meaning wasn't altogether clear, but I have kept editorial intrusions to a minimum and trust that those who have seen the taped interview will judge this a faithful presentation of its content.

*   *   *

In so far as one can define, explain or summarise the Deconstructionist project, one's account might go very briefly as follows. Deconstruction locates certain crucial oppositions or binary structures of meaning and value that constitute the discourse of 'Western metaphysics'. These include (among many others) the distinctions between form and content, nature and culture, thought and perception, essence and accident, mind and body, theory and practice, male and female, concept and metaphor, speech and writing etc. A Deconstructive reading then goes on to show how these terms are inscribed within a systematic structure of hierarchical privilege, such that one of each pair will always appear to occupy the sovereign or governing position. The aim is then to demonstrate – by way of close reading – how this system is undone, so to speak, from within; how the second or subordinate term in each pair has an equal (maybe a prior) claim to be treated as a *condition of possibility* for the entire system. Thus writing is regularly marginalised, denounced or put in its place – a strictly secondary, 'supplementary' place – by a long line of thinkers in the Western tradition, from Plato and Aristotle to Rousseau, Husserl, Saussure, Lévi-Strauss and the latter-day structuralist sciences of man. But just as often – as Derrida shows in *Of Grammatology* – writing resurfaces to assert its claim as the repressed other of this whole logocentric tradition, the 'wandering outcast', scapegoat or exile whose off-stage role is a precondition of the system. And this curious 'logic of supplementarity' operates wherever thinking is motivated by a certain constitutive need to exclude or deny that which makes it possible from the outset.

Now it is not hard to see how such a Deconstructive reading might affect the discourse of current (Post-Modern) architectural thought. Thus Peter Eisenman suggests that: 'the traditional opposition between structure and decoration, abstraction and figuration, figure and ground, form and function could be dissolved. Architecture could begin an exploration of the "between" within these categories.' And Derrida has likewise written of an architectural 'supplementarity', a movement of *différance* between and within concepts that would open up hitherto unthought-of inventive possibilities. The interview has a good deal to say about this in relation to Derrida's collaborative venture with Eisenman and Tschumi. His book *The Truth in Painting*

also has essays on Valeri, Adami and Titus-Carmel. In their work – as in Derrida's recent texts – one can make out the signs of a close and reciprocal exchange between Deconstruction and a certain problematics of writing and graphic representation. But critics have also applied the term 'Deconstruction' to other artists like Duchamp, Jasper Johns and Francis Bacon. Derrida himself makes mention of Magritte in the context of 'citationality' and the deconstruction of mimetic illusion through effects of juxtaposed image and text. And again there is his essay 'Restitutions' raising the question of painterly 'truth' by way of Meyer Schapiro's quarrel with Heidegger over the true significance of Van Gogh's *Old Shoes with Laces*, the question – seemingly so vital to each of them – as to who really owned those shoes.

So the interview asks what relation might exist between these various forms of deconstructive activity: that is to say – for want of better terms – 'creative' Deconstruction on the one hand, and diagnostic or critical commentary on the other. To pose the question like this is of course to fall back into just the kind of value-laden binary thinking that Deconstruction sets out to challenge. But it is equally mistaken to believe that, having once seen through their delusory appearance, one can finally come out on the far side of all such 'metaphysical' categories. What is required is a vigilant awareness of the way that they inhabit all our thinking about art, about criticism, philosophy and the human sciences, while also giving rise to problematic tensions within and between those disciplines.

In *The Truth in Painting* Derrida writes: 'We must sharpen the points, the blades or the edges of a certain *chiasmus*.' This figure – the trope of crossing or exchanged attributes – is one that plays an important role in his reading of Kant and the 'parergonal' discourse that frames Kant's thinking on questions of aesthetic judgement. It is also important to Eisenman, this and other tropes (like catachresis) that push beyond the bounds of reason or representation by radicalising language in its figural aspect. Thus Eisenman: 'the way to catachresis is not to suppress metaphor but to find the catachresis repressed in metaphor, and the way to another architecture is not to suppress the Classical but in fact to cut in . . . to surgically open up the Classical and the Modern to find what is repressed'. This interview may be read as an improvised commentary on the way that Deconstruction has opened up such questions for philosophy and the visual arts alike.

Christopher Norris

*   *   *

– Perhaps I could start by asking a perhaps rather naive question: can there be such a thing as 'Deconstructivist art' or indeed 'Deconstructivist architecture'? That is to say, do these terms refer to a given style, project or body of work? Or do they not rather signify a certain way of looking at various works and projects, a perception that would break with (or at least seek to challenge) established ideas of form, value and aesthetic representation?

Well, I don't know. . . I must say, when I first met, I won't say 'Deconstructive architecture', but the Deconstructive discourse on architecture, I was rather puzzled and suspicious. I thought at first that perhaps this was an analogy, a displaced discourse, and something more analogical than rigorous. And then – as I have explained somewhere – then I realised that on the contrary, the most efficient way of putting Deconstruction to work was by going through art and architecture. As you know, Deconstruction is not simply a matter of discourse or a matter of displacing the semantic content of the discourse, its conceptual structure or whatever. Deconstruction goes *through* certain social and political structures, meeting with resistance and displacing institutions as it does so. I think that in these forms of art, and in any architecture, to deconstruct traditional sanctions – theoretical, philosophical, cultural – effectively, you have to displace . . . I would say 'solid' structures, not only in the sense of material structures, but 'solid' in the sense of cultural, pedagogical, political, economic structures. And all the concepts which are, let us say, the target (if I may use this term) of Deconstruction, such as theology, the subordination of the sensible to the intelligible and so forth – these concepts are effectively displaced in order for them to become 'Deconstructive architecture'. That's why I am more and more interested in it, despite the fact that I am technically incompetent.

– Could you say a little more about your work with Bernard Tschumi and Peter Eisenman, and some of the collaborative projects under way in Paris at the moment?

Well, what I could do is just a narration of the way things happened. Once I had a phonecall from Bernard Tschumi, who I didn't know at the time, except by reputation. Tschumi told me: 'Some architects today are interested in your work and would you be interested in working with some of them, or one of them, on a project in La Villette?' As you know, Tschumi is responsible for all the architecture at La Villette. Of course I was surprised, but my answer was 'Why not?' And so I had my first encounter with Tschumi and I began to look at those projects and to read some texts, by Tschumi and Eisenman. Then I met Eisenman many times in New York. We worked together, we co-ordinated everything in discussion, and now there is a book which is soon to be published on these collaborations. My proposal was that we start with a text that I had recently written on Plato's *Timaeus* because it had to do with space, with Deconstruction, so to speak, 'in the universe'. It also had to do with a problem that I was interested in and that concerned, let us say, the *economic* determination of the way we usually read Plato. This strategic level was extremely important for me. So I gave this text to Peter Eisenman and in his own way he started a project that was correlated with but at the same time independent of my text. That was true collaboration – not 'using' the other's work, not just illustrating or selecting from it . . . and so there is a kind of discrepancy or, I would say, a productive dialogue between the concerns, the styles, the persons too. And so, after about 18 months' or two years' work, the project is now ready to be 'constructed', you might say. . . to be realised . . .

– So it would be wrong to see this as a new 'turn' in your thinking, a sudden recognition of connections, affinities or common points of interest between Deconstruction and the visual arts? In fact there are many passages in your earlier writing – and I am thinking here of texts like Force and Significance *or* Genesis and Structure *– where the argument turns on certain crucial (let us say) metaphors of an architectural provenance. The context here was your joint reading of the structuralist and phenomenological projects – more specifically, of Saussure and Husserl – as two, equally rigorous but finally incompatible reflections on the character of language and meaning. Thus you write: 'the relief and design of structures appears more clearly when content, which is the living energy of meaning, is neutralised. Somewhat like the architecture of an uninhabited or deserted city, reduced to its skeleton by some catastrophe of nature or art. A city no longer inhabited, not simply left behind, but haunted by meaning and culture'. And of course these architectural figures and analogies occur more often in your later writings on Kant and the tradition of Classical aesthetics (for instance, 'The Parergon' in* The Truth in Painting). *Thus for Kant,* architectonic *is defined as the 'art of systems', that which articulates the various orders of truth-claim and ensures their proper (hierarchical) relationship one with another. So in a sense one could argue that your work has always been crucially concerned with 'architectural' models and metaphors. Do you perceive a clear continuity there, or am I just imagining all this?*

No, not at all. But I would like to say something about the concept of analogy or metaphor you rightly used a moment ago. Of course there is a lot of architectural metaphor, not only in my texts but in the whole philosophical tradition. And Deconstruction – the word Deconstruction – sounds very much like such a metaphor, an architectural metaphor. But I think that it's more complex than that, since the word appeared or was underlined in a certain situation where structuralism was dominant on the scene. So Deconstruction shared certain motifs with the structuralist project while at the same time attacking that project. . . .

But Deconstruction doesn't mean that we have to stay within those architectural metaphors. It doesn't mean, for example, that we have to destroy something which is built – physically built or culturally built or theoretically built – just in order to reveal a naked ground on which something new could be built. Deconstruction is perhaps a way of questioning this architectural model itself – the architectural model which is a general question, even within philosophy, the metaphor of foundations, of superstructures, what Kant calls 'architectonic' etc, as well as the concept of the *arche* . . . So Deconstruction means also the putting into question of architecture in philosophy and perhaps architecture itself.

When I discovered what we now call 'Deconstructive architecture' I was interested in the fact that these architects were in fact deconstructing the essentials of tradition, and were criticising everything that subordinated architecture to something else – the value of, let's say, usefulness or beauty or living – '*habite*' – etc – not in order to build something else that would be useless or ugly or uninhabitable, but to free architecture from all those external finalities, extraneous goals. And not in order to reconstitute some pure and original architecture – on the contrary, just to put architecture in communication with other media, other arts, to *contaminate* architecture . . . And notice that in my way of dealing with Deconstruction I suspect the *concept* of metaphor itself, in so far as it involves a complicated network of philosophemes, a network that would always lead us back at some point into architecture . . .

– Yes, this is a topic you raise in your Fifty-Two Aphorisms for a Forward. *There you explicitly disown the idea that Deconstruction is in any sense an 'architectural metaphor', a figure that would serve obliquely to name or to specify some ongoing project in the field of building and design. And this for the reason, as you say, that it is 'no longer possible to make use of the concept of metaphor'. But might we not say with equal force (as you did some years ago in 'White Mythology') that there is no possibility of doing without some residual 'concept of metaphor'; that if indeed all concepts come down to metaphors – as Nietzsche argued – then it is also the case that we possess only concepts of metaphor, ideas that have always already been worked over by the discourse of philosophic reason, from Aristotle on? I take this argument as one more example of the firm insistence, on your part, that 'Deconstruction' is not be treated as a break with 'Western metaphysics', a leap outside the logocentric tradition that thinks to land on some alternative, radically different ground. Is it not this acceptance of the need to work patiently within and against the structures of inherited thought that has chiefly distinguished Deconstruction from other, less exacting and rigorous forms of Post-Modern thought? I ask this question – as you may by now have guessed – in the hope that you will be drawn into offering some account of what specifically sets Deconstruction apart from the broader Post-Modern project.*

As you know, I never use the word 'post', the prefix 'post'; and I have many reasons for this. One of those reasons is that this use of the prefix implies a periodisation or an epochalIsation which is highly problematic for me. Then again, the word 'post' implies that something is highly finished – that we can get rid of what went *before* Deconstruction, and I don't think anything of the sort. For instance, to go back to the first point of your question, I don't believe that the opposition between concept and metaphor can ever be erased. I have never suggested that all concepts were simply metaphors, or that we couldn't make use of that distinction, because in fact at the end of that essay

['White Mythology'] I deconstruct this argument also, and I say that we need. for scientific reasons and many reasons, to keep this distinction at work. So this is a very complicated gesture.

Now as for architecture, I think that *Deconstruction* comes about - let us carry on using this word to save time – when you have deconstructed some architectural philosophy, some architectural assumptions – for instance, the hegemony of the aesthetic, of beauty, the hegemony of usefulness, of functionality, of living, of dwelling. But then you have to *reinscribe* these motifs within the work. You can't (or you shouldn't) simply dismiss those values of dwelling, functionality, beauty and so on. You have to construct, so to speak, a new space and a new form, to shape a new way of building in which those motifs or values are reinscribed, having meanwhile lost their external hegemony. The inventiveness of powerful architects consists I think in this reinscription, the economy of this reinscription, which involves also some respect for tradition, for memory. Deconstruction is not simply forgetting the past. What has dominated theology or architecture or anything else is still there, in some way, and the inscriptions, the, let's say, *archive* of these deconstructed structures, the archive should be as readable as possible, as legible as we can make it. That is the way I try to write or to teach. And I think the same is true, to some extent, in architecture.

– You have stressed your suspicion of 'post-' movements in philosophy and art, whether Post-Modernist, Post-Structuralist, or post-humanist (as in your early essay ' The Ends of Man'). And this for the reason – as I take it – that all steps beyond *in the name of this or that radical new way of thinking are liable to find themselves unwittingly reinscribed within the terms of that same oppositional order of thought which they hope thereby to escape. Do you not see a risk of something similar happening with current attempts to break with the so-called 'Modernist' paradigm and its associated structure of concepts and values? Thus Peter Eisenman: 'For architecture to enter a post-Hegelian condition, it must move away from the rigidity and value-structure of these dialectical oppositions.' (ie figure and ground, ornament and structure, form and function etc). Or would it perhaps be true to say – as some like Gregory Ulmer have claimed – that things have moved on during the past decade or so from 'Deconstruction' as a species of meticulous textual critique to 'applied grammatology' as a practice of creative reinscription that goes beyond such basic, preliminary work? Would this be borne out by what you have recently achieved in your collaborative enterprise with artists like Eisenman and Tschumi, or would you perhaps consider this a wrong understanding, a false opposition?*

I wouldn't say 'false' opposition. It is an opposition which I would say, is pertinent for some forms of appropriation in so far as it amounts to a critical method within texts, within literary texts or even philosophical texts. But I insisted from the beginning that Deconstruction was not *simply* a method, was not a critique, or not simply critical. The concept of critique or criticism is deconstructive somewhere... It is not negative – it was linked from the beginning with affirmation, with the 'yes', an affirmation which is not a 'position' in the Hegelian sense. So the move which is described by Greg Ulmer is not so much a move *in* Deconstruction. It is a move we can identify in some places – I wouldn't say 'in' my work, from that point of view at least. And of course the variety of fields, of disciplines, of texts, of publishers – this variety was necessary from the outset, philosophical and literary texts and painting and now architecture and some others too. legal texts and many other things.

So I think it is important, this way of opening up the boundaries, and mainly the academic boundaries between texts and disciplines; and when I say academic boundaries I'm thinking not only of the humanistic disciplines and philosophy, but also of architecture – the teaching of architecture. This crossing, this going through the boundaries of disciplines, is one of the main – not just strategems but *necessities* of Deconstruction. The grafting of one art on to another, the contamination of codes, the dissemination of contexts, are sometimes 'methods'

or 'strategems' of Deconstruction, but most importantly they are moments of what we call history. And that is why I don't think Deconstruction belongs to an epoch or a period, even a modern one.

I don't think Deconstruction is something specifically modern. There are some 'modern' features of what we identify as Deconstruction in some academic contexts, but what makes Deconstruction *unavoidable* has been at work a long time, even with Plato or Descartes. So we have to distinguish between, let us say, some phenomena which are not the entirety of Deconstruction and which give rise to methods, to teaching, to thematic treatment, and something more hidden, more persistent, less amenable to system or method which makes this thematic Deconstruction possible in discourse and in teaching and the arts.

– Isn't it a problem that the term 'Modernism' (let alone 'Post-Modernism') means such very different things for philosophers on the one hand, and literary critics or art-historians on the other? And doesn't Deconstruction need to adopt a somewhat different stance with regard to these two phenomena? I am thinking here of your recent essays on Kant, on the 'Principle of Reason', and on the Enlightenment tradition in general. There you make it plain that we cannot simply break with that tradition; that any criticism must come (so to speak) from inside and avail itself of the concepts and categories of enlightened critique while questioning their claims to ultimate truth. And I think this places some considerable distance between your own thinking and the kinds of project pursued by [for instance] Lyotard or Baudrillard Whereas the Post-Modern 'turn' in literature, art and cultural theory has a different set of historical coordinates and a different relation to issues of truth. reason and ideological critique. Haven't these distinctions become rather blurred in recent debate?

I wouldn't want to call Deconstruction a critique of modernity. But neither is it 'modern' or in any sense a glorification of modernity. It is very premature to venture these generalisations, these concepts of period. I would say that I just don't know what these categories mean, except that of course I can tell more or less what other people mean them to signify ... But for me they are not rigorous concepts. Nor is Deconstruction a unitary *concept*. although it is often deployed in that way, a usage that I find very disconcerting... Sometimes I prefer to say deconstructions in the plural, just to be careful about the heterogeneity and the multiplicity, the necessary multiplicity of gestures. of fields, of styles. Since it is not a system, not a method, it cannot be homogenised. Since it takes the singularity of every context into account, Deconstruction is different from one context to another. So I should certainly want to reject the idea that 'Deconstruction' denotes any theory, method or univocal concept. Nevertheless it must denote *something*. something that can at least be recognised in its working or its effects. . .

Of course this doesn't mean that Deconstruction *is* that 'something', or that you can find Deconstruction everywhere. So on the one hand we have to define some working notion, some regulative concept of Deconstruction. But it is very difficult to gather this in a simple formula. I know that the enemies of Deconstruction say: 'Well, since you cannot offer a definition then it must be an obscure concept and you must be an obscurantist thinker'. To which I would respond that Deconstruction is first and foremost a suspicion directed against just that kind of thinking – 'what is ...?' 'what is the essence of ...?' and so on.

– Could we perhaps take that point a bit further? Some theorists of the Post-Modern (Charles Jencks among them) have rejected what they see as the negative, even 'nihilist' implications of the Deconstruction movement in contemporary art. According to Jencks, 'Architecture is essentially constructive. It builds up structures, depends or joint endeavours of mutual confidence, the combination of foresight, good-will and investment – all of which Deconstruction undermines, if not totally destroys.' I thought you might like to comment on this and similar responses, especially in view of current debates – taken up in the American and British press – about the 'politics of Decon-

struction' and its supposed nihilist leanings. I'm sure you would say that they have misunderstood.

Absolutely, absolutely. . . There has been much criticism, many objections that we find in the newspapers, in the bad newspapers . . . Which doesn't just mean that the people who write such things are jealous. Often they are academics who don't read the many texts in which not only I but many people insist on the fact that Deconstruction is *not* negative, is not nihilistic. Of course it goes through the experience and the questioning of what nihilism is. Of course, of course. And who knows what nihilism is or isn't? Even the people who object don't raise the question 'What is nihilism?' Nevertheless, Deconstruction is or should be an affirmation linked to promises, to involvement, to responsibility. As you know, it has become more and more concerned with these concepts – even Classical concepts – of responsibility, affirmation and commitment . . . So when people say it's negative, nihilistic and so forth, either they don't read or they are arguing in bad faith. But this can and should be analysed . . .

– In the Aphorisms *you refer to an 'ageless contract' that has always existed between architecture and a certain idea of dwelling or habitation. And of course this points toward Heidegger and a whole thematics of building, dwelling, and poetic thinking. You also remark – in a slightly different but related context – that 'there is no inhabitable place for the aphorism', that is to say, no place within the kind of large-scale conceptual edifice that philosophy has traditionally taken for its home. Thus: 'the aphorism is neither a house, nor a temple, nor a school, nor a parliament, nor an* agora, *nor a tomb. Neither a pyramid nor, above all, a stadium. What else?' Could I ask you to pursue this particular line of thought in whatever direction you wish, and perhaps suggest also what connections it might have with your latest writings on Heidegger?*

Ah, that's a very difficult question . . .

– Yes, I'm sorry . . .

No, no, not at all. Difficult questions are necessary. The fact that architecture has always been interpreted as dwelling, or the element of dwelling – dwelling for human beings or dwelling for the gods – the place where gods or people are present or gathering or living or so on. Of course this is a very profound and strong interpretation, but one which first submits architecture, what we call architecture or the art of building, to a value which can be questioned. In Heidegger such values are linked with the question of building, with the theme of, let's say, keeping, conserving, watching over, etc. And I was interested in questioning those assumptions in Heidegger, asking what this might amount to, an architecture that wouldn't be simply subordinated to those values of habitation, dwelling, sheltering the presence of gods and human beings. Would it be possible? Would it still be an architecture? I think that what people like Eisenman and Tschumi have shown me – people who call themselves Deconstructivist architects – is that this is indeed possible; not possible as a *fact*, as a matter of simple demonstration, because of course you can always perceive their architecture as again giving place to dwelling, sheltering, etc; because the question I am asking now is not only the question of what they build, but of how we interpret what they build. Of course we can interpret in a very traditional way – viewing this as simply a 'modern' transformation of the same old kinds of architecture. So Deconstruction is not simply an activity or commitment on the part of the architect; it is also on the part of people who read, who look at these buildings, who enter the space, who move in the space, who experience the space in a different way. From this point of view I think that the architectural experience (let's call it that, rather than talking about 'buildings' as such) . . . what they offer is precisely the chance of experiencing the possibility of these inventions of a different architecture, one that wouldn't be, so to speak, 'Heideggerian' . . .

– The Aphorisms *have a good deal to say about the International College of Philosophy and its work in promoting inter-disciplinary exchange. They also make a point of not talking about 'projects' in this or that field, as if the work undertaken could be staked out in advance,* or in accordance with some governing scheme or teleology. Thus you write, in Aphorism 36: *'To say that it does not have a project does not amount to denouncing its empiricism or its adventurism. In the same way an architecture without a project is engaged perhaps in a more thoughtful, more inventive, more propitious work . . .'*

Could you say something more about the kinds of new and productive thinking that have emerged from this bringing-together of people from hitherto separate disciplines? Just what goes on when you 'exchange ideas' – to put it very crudely – with artists like Eisenman or Bernard Tschumi; an enterprise without clear-cut aims and ambitions, without some teleological goal?

I was referring to the French meaning of the word 'project' in the code of architecture. I don't know whether it has the same meaning in English. A project is something which is prior to the work, which has its own economy, a governing role which can then be applied and developed . . . And you have the same kind of relation between the project, or the concept, and its carrying-out in practice as between, say, the transcendental signified and its incarnation in the body, in writing etc. So there is a critical reflection on this concept of the 'project' going on among a number of French architects. When I say there is no project in the College, I don't mean to say that we start without any idea of where we're going, but that the relation between the project and the experience, the act, has no Classical or philosophical equivalent. For instance, the College could be seen from one aspect as having the character of a new foundation. And of course a 'foundation' is something with strong philosophical, as well as architectural links. It has its building, its forms, its shape, its place . . . But in fact, within this College we ask questions – sometimes, not always, in a deconstructive way – about what grounding means, what the foundation means, what the space of the community means, what hierarchy means, in terms not only of academic authority but also in terms of the pedagogical scenography, the organisation of the classroom, the way we appoint people, elect people, the way the hierarchies are stabilised or destabilised, and so forth. And all these things have their architectural models. So since our model was not the Western university as it is organised now, or the philosophy that lies behind this modern university (or modern Western university), we had to invent also the symbolic and physical architecture of this new community without referring to any previous, given model.

Of course all the time we have to negotiate, we have to compromise with previous, given models – that's the political strategy, and I think that architects also have to negotiate with norms and practical constraints and so on. Nevertheless, these tactics are oriented toward something that would be new, or that would bring about a real alteration in the old structure. And I think that from the beginning we had, my friends and I, this certainty that first it was something new – something new to be built in the architectural sense, new commitments, a new space, a new field of knowledge . . . But also, more specifically, the sense that we *had to* work with architects, that the teaching and experience of architecture would be an important aspect of our work at the College. So even though my collaboration with Eisenman and Tschumi was not officially a part of the programme, it had to do with the College and indeed gave rise to various conferences, meetings and communications . . . events that led on to a close involvement between philosophers and architects. The one for which I wrote my *Aphorisms* was an example of it.

– You have talked about the relationship between 'modernity' in art, architecture, philosophy etc, and a certain idea of the modern university, one that took hold in Germany a couple of centuries back and which still exerts a great influence on the way we think about disciplines, subject-areas, questions of intellectual competence, and so forth. And this would perhaps take us back to what you said previously about Kant's 'architectonic', his doctrine of the faculties, that which enforces a proper separation of realms between pure and practical reason, theoretical understanding, aesthetic judgment and their various modalities or powers . . . To some extent your work in the

International College is a way of deconstructing those relations, showing how they give rise to endless litigation or boundary-disputes, often played out in very practical terms as a matter of institutional politics . . .

Oh yes, I agree with your definition of what is going on. Deconstructing not only theoretically, not only giving signals of the process at work, but trying to deconstruct in a practical fashion, that is, to set up and build new structures implying this work of Deconstruction. It's not easy, and it is never done in or through a single gesture. It takes a long time and involves some very complicated gestures. It is always unfinished, heterogeneous, and I think there is no such thing as a 'pure' Deconstruction or a deconstructive project that is finished or completed.

– Isn't there a risk that Deconstruction might become mixed up with that strain of Post-Modern or neo-pragmatist thought which says that philosophy is just a 'kind of writing', on a level with poetry, criticism or the 'cultural conversation of mankind'? That these distinctions are merely 'rhetorical' or imposed by an obsolete 'enlightenment' doctrine of the faculties, so that we had best get rid of them and abandon any notion of philosophy as having its own special interests, distinctive truth-claims, conceptual history or whatever? Do you see that as a constant risk?

There are many risks and this is one of them. Sometimes it is an interesting risk, sometimes it opens doors and spaces in the fields which are trying to protect themselves from Deconstruction. But once the door is open, then you have to make things more specific, and I would say, following your suggestion, that no indeed, philosophy is not *simply* a 'kind of writing'; philosophy has a very rigorous specificity which has to be respected, and it is a very hard discipline with its own requirements, its own autonomy, so that you cannot simply mix philosophy with literature, with painting, with architecture. There is a point you can recognise, some opening of the various contexts (including the philosophical context) that makes Deconstruction possible. But it still requires a rigorous approach, one that would situate this opening in a strict way, that would organise, so to speak, this contamination or this grafting without losing sight of those specific requirements. So I am very suspicious – and this is not just a matter of idiosyncracy or a matter of training – I am very suspicious of the over-easy mixing of discourses to which your question referred. On the contrary, Deconstruction pays the greatest attention to multiplicity, to heterogeneity, to these sharp and irreducible differences. If we don't want to homogenise eveything then we have to respect the specificity of discourses, especially that of philosophical discourse.

– There is one particular essay of yours which I think may help to focus some of these questions. It is called 'Of an Apocalyptic Tone Recently Adopted in Philosophy', a title that you borrow (or cite) verbatim from Kant, and it strikes me that there are two very different things going on throughout this text. In fact it is often hard to know whether you are writing, as it were, 'in your own voice' or whether the passage in question is sous rature *or to be read as if placed within quotation-marks. Sometimes you write of the need to maintain 'Enlightenment' values, to preserve what you call the 'lucid vigil' of Enlightenment critique and truth. In this sense the essay appears to side with Kant against the adepts, the mystagogues, the fake illuminati, those who*

would claim an immediate or self-present access to truth by virtue of their own 'inner light', without submitting their claims to the democratic parliament of the faculties. Elsewhere you adopt your own version of the 'apocalyptic tone' – a series of injunctions, apostrophes, speech-acts or performatives of various kinds – as if to defend the right of these characters not to go along with Kant's rules for the proper, self-regulating conduct of philosophic discourse. It does seem to me a profoundly ambivalent essay. On the one hand it is establishing a distance – even an antagonism – between Deconstruction and the discourse of Enlightenment critique. On the other it is saying that the Kantian project is somehow indispensable, that it is bound up with the very destiny of thought in our time, that we cannot simply break with it as certain Post-Modernist thinkers would wish – or have I misread your essay in some fairly basic way?

No, no, you read it very well. I agree with everything you said. It is a very, very ambivalent essay. I tried – as I often do – to achieve and say many things at once. Of course I am 'in favour' of the Enlightenment; I think we shouldn't simply leave it behind us, so I want to keep this tradition alive. But at the same time I know that there are certain historical forms of Enlightenment, certain things in this tradition that we need to criticise or to deconstruct. So it is sometimes in the name of, let us say, a *new* Enlightenment that I deconstruct a given Enlightenment. And this requires some very complex strategies; requires that we should let many voices speak . . . There is nothing monological, no monologue – that's why the responsibility for Deconstruction is never individual or a matter of the single, self-privileged authorial voice. It is always a multiplicity of voices, of gestures . . . And you can take this as a rule: that each time Deconstruction speaks through a single voice, it's wrong, it is not 'Deconstruction' any more. So in this particular essay, as you rightly said a moment ago, not only do I let many voices speak at the same time, but the problem is precisely that multiplicity of voices, that variety of tones, within the *same* utterance or indeed the same word or syllable, and so on. So that's the question. That's one of the questions.

But of course today the political, ideological consequences of the Enlightenment are still very much with us – and very much in need of questioning. So a 'new' enlightenment, to be sure, which may mean Deconstruction in its most active or intensive form, and not what we inherited in the name of *Aufklärung*, critique, *siècle des lumières* and so forth. And as you know, these are already very different things. So we have to remember this.

– I suppose I'm looking for some kind of equivalence between what we call 'Modernism' in philosophy, let's say Kantian philosophy, and the term 'Modernism' as conventionally applied in architecture and the visual arts. You might compare the attitude that Deconstructivist architects take toward Modernism – not simply one of rejection or supercession, but a critical attitude directed toward that particular form of Modernist critique . . .

Of course. That's why I'm reluctant to say that Deconstruction is Modern or Post-Modern. But I should also be reluctant to say that it's not Modern, or that it's anti-Modern, or anti-Post-Modern. I wouldn't want to say that what is Deconstructive, if there is such a thing, is specifically Modern or Post-Modern. So we have to be very careful with the use of these epithets.

— * —

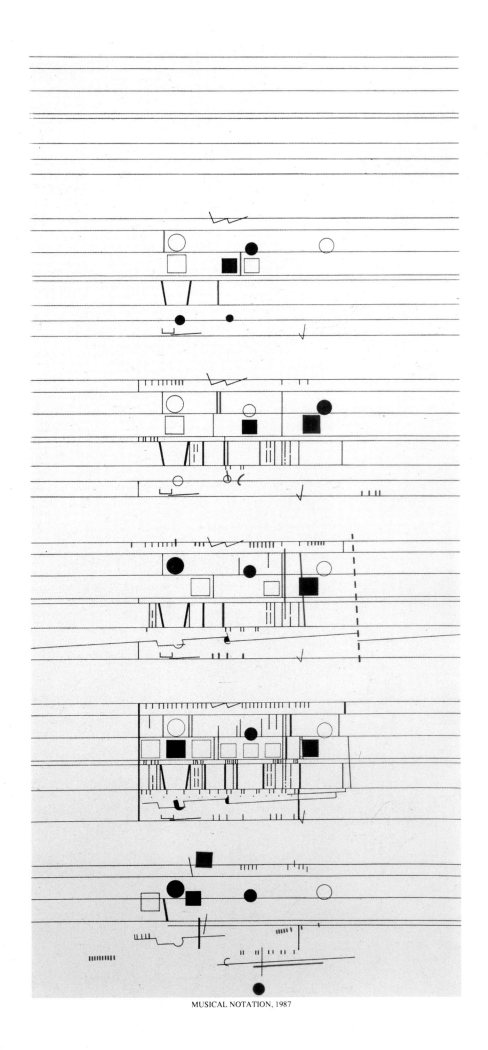

MUSICAL NOTATION, 1987

BERNARD TSCHUMI
Projects for Tokyo and Strasbourg

PERSPECTIVE DRAWING, 1987

New National Theatre of Japan, Tokyo

Hypothesis

How to deconstruct opera and architecture so as to 'think' their concepts and simultaneously to observe them from an external and detached point of view? How to devise a configuration of concepts which is systematic and irreducible, that each concept intervenes at some decisive moment of the work? How to question the unity of a building without recourse either to a composition of articulated and formalised elements or to a random accumulation of isolated programmatic fragments? To play on limits without being enclosed within limits? To relate to other operas while referring only to one's own?

Juxtaposition

We have therefore abandoned traditional rules of composition and harmony, replacing them with an organisation based on breaking apart the traditional components of theatre and opera

house and developing a new 'tonality' or 'sound'. No more artful articulations between auditorium, stage, foyer, grand staircase; instead, a new pleasure through the parallel juxtaposition of indeterminate cultural meanings, as opposed to fixed historicist practices.

Functional constraints are not translated into a composition of symbolic units, but are extrapolated into a score of programmatic strips, analogous to the lines of a musical score, each containing the main activities and related spaces. The sequence is as follows:

A: The glass avenue provides access; its busy mezzanines (theatre lobbies) act as a vertical spectacle, while its ground floor gathers crowds using the public services.

B: The vertical foyers overlook the glass avenue and encompass cloakrooms, box offices, bars or buffets, suspended gardens.

C: The auditoriums act as an acoustic strip accommodating each audience in a minimum

of volume (for acoustic quality) and a maximum of visual comfort.

D: The servicing strip as a central artery.

E: The stages provide maximum flexibility and technical possibilities.

F: The backstage area.

G: The dressing rooms and related spaces – organised along the balconies of a four-storey artists' concourse (to avoid anonymous repetition of corridors).

The insertion of programmatic events into architecture is a means of breaking down or deconstructing its traditional components. The deconstructed elements can be manipulated independently, according to conceptual, narrative or programmatic concerns (just as the violin can be made independent from the piano in a concerto). Thus the juxtaposition of each band can lead to intensified operatic effects: the layering of multiple facts as well as their interpretation.

13

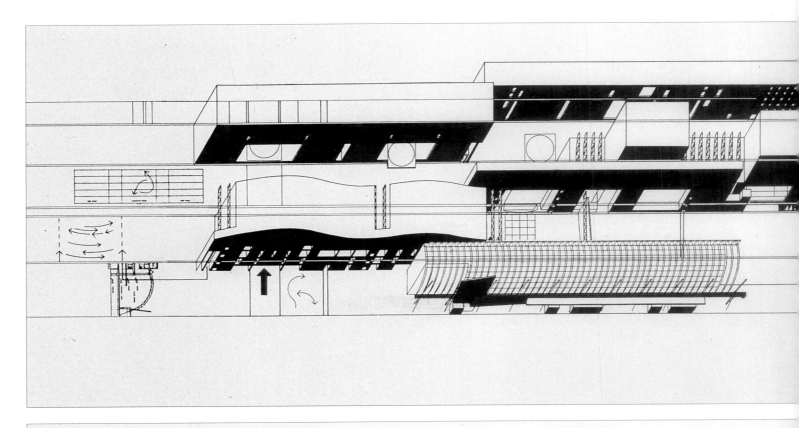

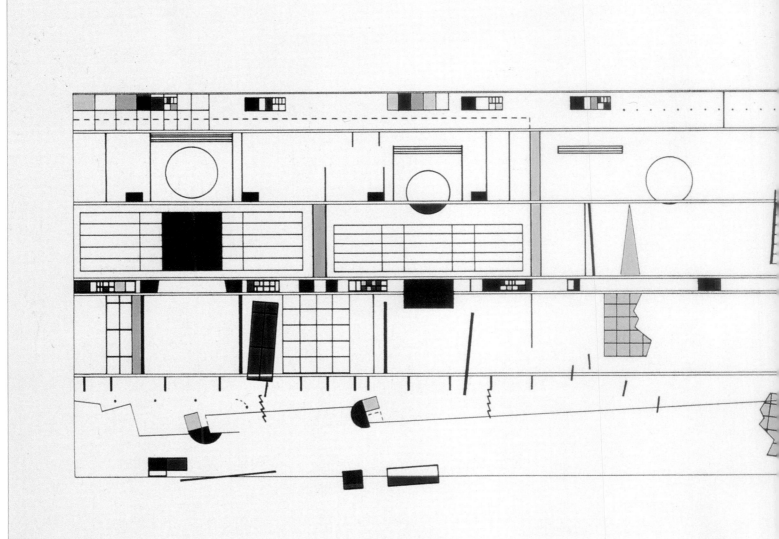

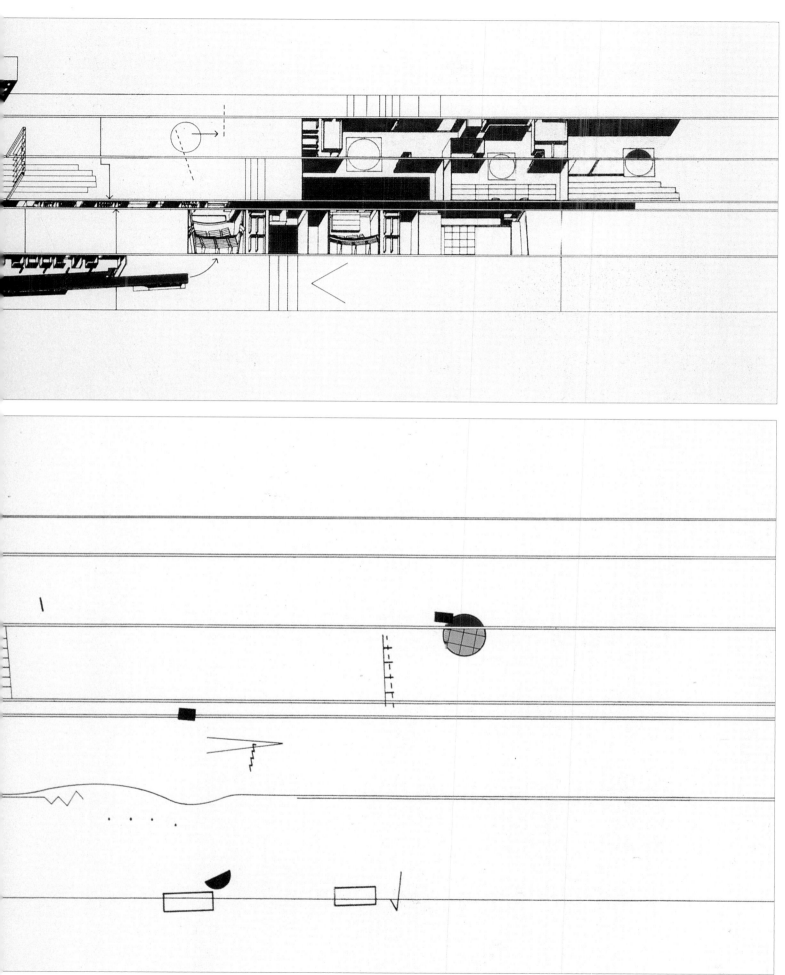

BELOW: PLANAR NOTATION, 1987

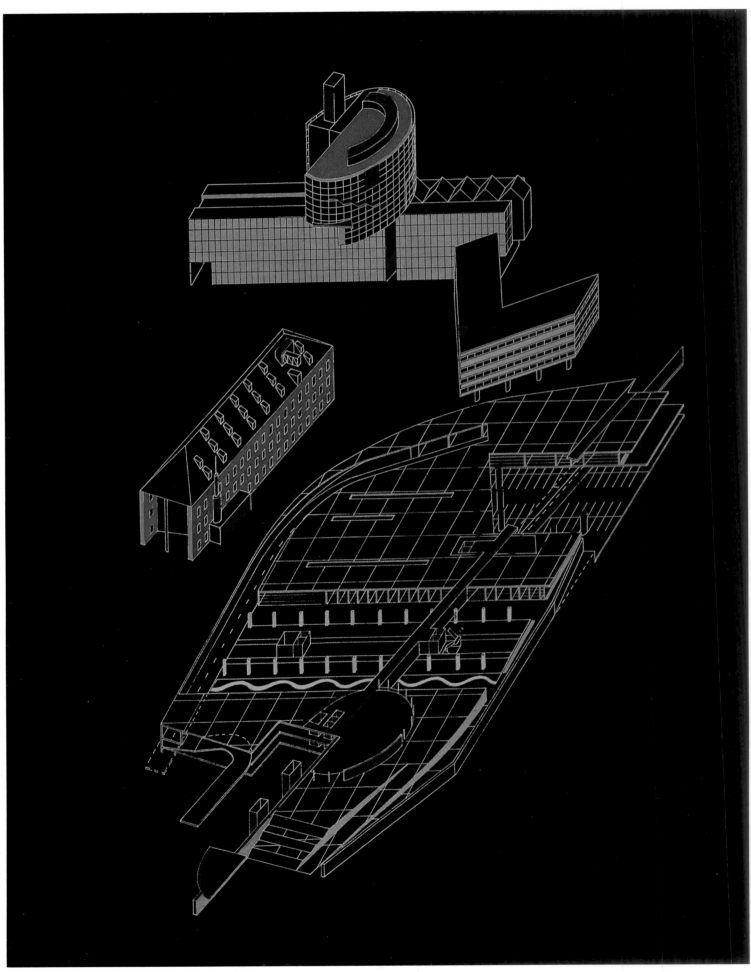

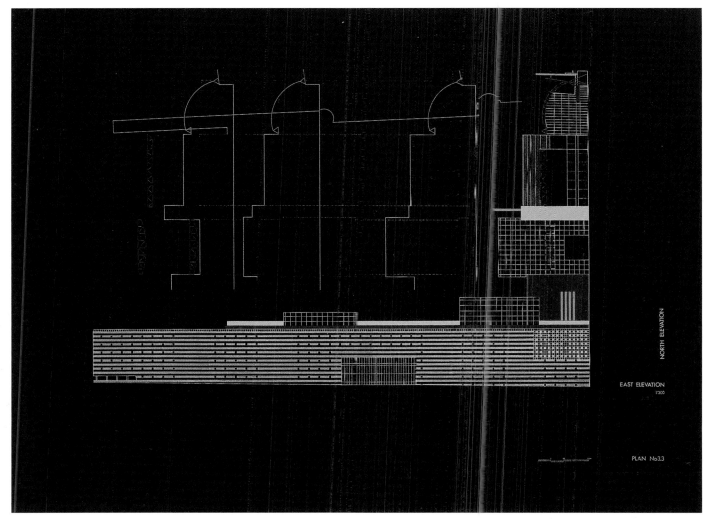

NORTH ELEVATION

EAST ELEVATION
1:300

PLAN No.3

PLAN WITH EAST AND NORTH ELEVATIONS

New County Hall, Strasbourg

The proposed location is southwest of the town, on the bank of the river Ill, where historic Strasbourg (known as 'Little France') meets the Strasbourg of the 20th century ('the slabs of the Medical Faculty'). Before it stands a dam built by Vauban, and remains of the fortifications are still visible. The brief asked for a representative building, and seemed to favour the demolition of the disused 18th-century building at the entrance to the site, the large mansard roof of which acts as a visual link between the historic town and the new districts.

The question of demolition was fundamental. To demolish an interesting building, a major landmark of the town, simply to make room for an essentially adminstrative building suggests a certain cynicism. It seemed that a more up-to-date approach would be to reject this expedient and introduce a new concept of urban combination.

It is important to remember that the site lies exactly on the boundary between two types of urban planning, one emphasising the traditional perimeter block, the other reflecting the ideology of large postwar developments, in which each building is an isolated entity. Rather than imitate either, we adopted a conceptual framework that would create a new relation between these different architectural types and offer a strategy that could be applied to similar situations.

Strasbourg has witnessed a variety of urban layouts – Roman, medieval, Neo-Classical compositions of the 18th-century, 19th-century German town planning, and the counter-compositions of Van Doesburg. Consequently, we decided the nature of the competition site as a meeting-point between old and new could both justify the rehabilitation of the old barracks and suggest a new urban project that would clarify the role of the historical frag-

ments in relation to the contemporary period.

The fragments

The problem, then, was to design a complex of offices linking the old and the new. Fragmentation seemed appropriate for the following reasons: First, the fragment makes it possible to take into account the specific constraints of each element of the brief (eg the conference hall) without compromising the whole (eg repetitive floors of offices). Second, the fragment allows all the elements to be autonomous, while making it easier to perceive their relative importance. Third, the varying scale of each fragment makes it possible to relate the uncohesive space of the 20th-century buildings with the cohesive space of the historic town. Fourth, the fragment also makes it possible, by suggesting free juxtapositions, to achieve a spatial invention, a poetic dimension and a new conception of the site.

17

ABOVE: GROUND-FLOOR PLA N

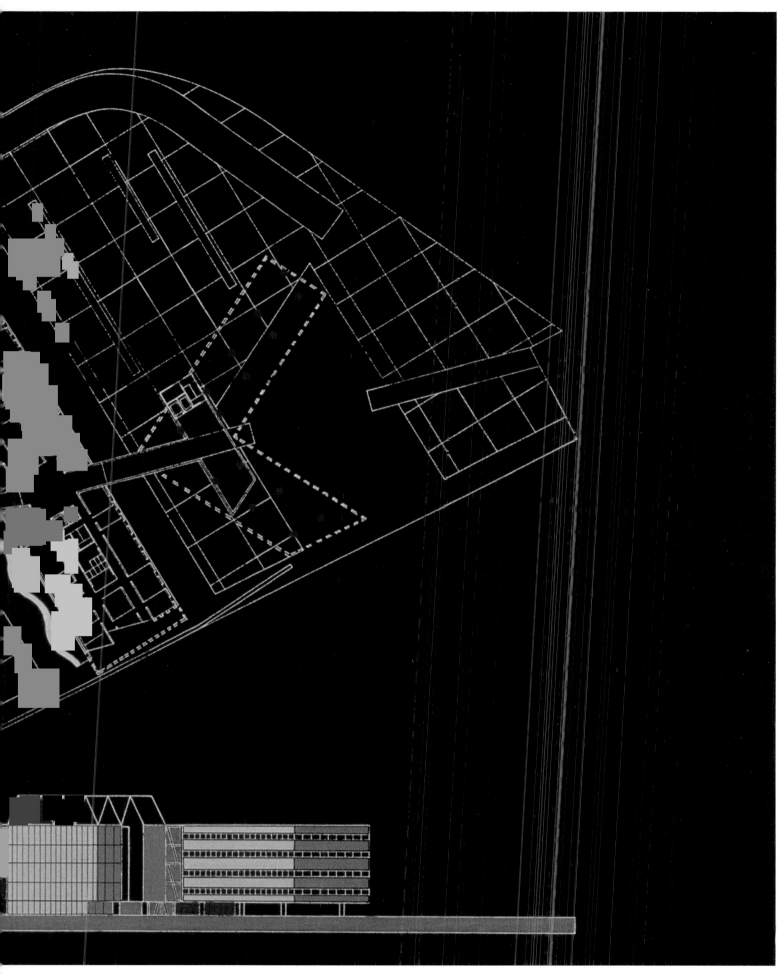

DANIEL LIBESKIND
Still Life with Red Predictions

BERLIN 'CITY EDGE', 'MEMORIAL TO MIES', AM KARLSBAD

Letalin will fly back, without Ulalume.

Sharp staccato sounds will bypass Cerebrus barking, *sui juris*, at the stranger in us; will be transmitted by heredity to the abracadabra violoncello playing a solo motet in slow neon without the bow, without the cello.

Odours creating the illusion of rotating, difficult to taste conventions will ripple the water already agitated by a continual barrage of ancient texts thrown into it. Both odour and water will become things permanently verging on spinning, like the Ring. A similar example in metal: wilful arcs of polished motel siding fused with astral fibres will be used for making discus or the shield protecting local poverty from being beaten up by an alien ratio.

One will acquire a funny hypnotic power over flattened minds, particularly those of stupid museum curators who reject ornithological art because it is influenced by Chopin's flighty spirit. One will censor the invisible writings by General Petain which hide in the delicate Art Nouveau ornament of the Metropolitain – provided one is willing to reconnoitre a flat cladophyll with a feeling of remorse.

Inside each piece of furniture – even tall ones – there will be a play performed. A delicate young lad in the dead of winter will be able to participate in a sensory-ritual quest for lost birch, pine and linden trees now replaced by single-fit smells of ionisation exclusively designed to furnish each living room with rapid, national bursts of sneezing. Tulips anyone?

Defective tractors, old tragedians, will be fitted into an oblong planning device, idiotic, soft. The suggestion that 'lately the future is appealing only to actors who can kill their audience without a licence' will become a source of inspiration to many. Farming will be illegal, pleasant.

(Ibn in Arabic, Ben in Hebrew, and so on.) Preface the lament with Beelzebub's concern for spicy Amontillado, a phenomenal offer. Tip. Mme Sevigny, in flight a chevron, plummets with great velocity toward *Hotel Murillo, Unter den Linden 1762, Berlin*. Tip. And even more:

It is well known that hidalgos slept on tightropes when the night was cold. Certain snoring sounds were labelled as repulsive when their musculature contracted to a sixth of its size with the sound 'shhhh . . .' – fickle power when tacitly negotiating for deep sleep with an owl! Vishnu, called the Preserver, believed that popular tradition had an odd number of knees – demanded that the sempiternal drip through a sieve without tying the carcass to an incarnation on wheels or increasing timidity enormously. The body's largest arrested organ: skin.

Indigence, an advantage without talent. The Sphinx killed herself though the deception perpetrated was half human, half Nordic or the sculptor's mumbo-jumbo. Must every fault be brought to silence by solitude? Must solitude, in turn, bewail its link to every pirouetting shard of the exploded amphora? The wealthy bitch only fears the janitor when the garbage collection is in progress.

The last letter of the first story must have been the first letter of the last story since Egyptians spoke a Hebrew dialect whenever they inserted a scarab into their mouth to simulate a circumcision best performed in secret. The rage for randomly selected victims has softened those who are still lingering in bed.

Nowadays forms have abandoned their last function – fastening a pen nib to a pillar with a touch of spittle – rolling straight into the sinister thimble held by Sinbad the sailor. Who will decypher, save and entertain purple hostility? Poems will be readily available if you call the right number or pull the lip all the way down till it touches the element. Fencing will become a fashionable sort. Dangling in a loophole will seem as interesting as artificial onions to allow a couple of others in without discomfort thus disproving that incarnation alone is capable of emptying the destination of its meaning. Anyone can fit into an imaginary three-dimensional envelope provided one is hollow, ie, fully two-directional.

20

The Surface Must Die. A Proof

Eve, holly, ivy, apple. There will be no more cities on the surface only what is unfinished: ugly men, tours of Ellis Island, the Other. Even one's own mother tends to become cruel when one has interest in childhood, particularly early puberty. Meanwhile Reality is played by Major Leaguers using zero as a wall and nothing for a bat – while pretending that the Manager napping in the bleachers is the ball. The baseball game of dimensions, prophetically shielded by trouble-free membranes made out of poetic opacity, converts ambiguous identity into unequivocal yes-content. Yet if you depend on the internal reserves lodged inside the dim shrine some will call you a pig deposited in precise manner by representation; others will accuse you of being demented because you trust every indication – internal or not – which dangles like a *persona non grata* from the Tree of Life. Gloss over the geometry of silence thrown under every *foglio di carta*!

The line is always perpendicular to a vibration emitted by Dio who first kissed triangles, then became equilateral, circular, finally a repository of tradition in liquid. Drunk Castillians still consider the Vertical a form panacea because it provides God with an old-folks' home, ie, a mild *cannot*. This little hypothesis confirms that revelations always belong to some Ann, Cathy or Eve.

If you see the crossed out I as letter K or consider dollars a fearful code (curve and two parallel lines) you are likely to uproot infinity overtaking in the NO PASSING lane. I said before that the Real is a pigeon but what I meant is that its physiognomy nestles softly and flexibly along the region where verbs can dissemble their filial position. Nails, for one, are part of the frame yet also appear in it especially when a T shakes itself into postulates. (I quote this from a fine, empty piece of imported information for the benefit of the mob with a proviso it reconsider. The watch dial is an example of a figure that all slaves already symbolise in practice.)

Definitions originate midway between the tail and one hundred and twenty degree coloratura space. Wings are distended round awe not dull house space. When the feasible expires in triangulation magic highlights the congenitally three-pointed eye. You are fountain on right, serve premonition on left, usurp the mental. Facts befuddle the elongated person who has returned from this hay-ride with two *whys*. By allowing loosely jointed equivalence to mediate the sleeper's indefinite extension into dreams one can bless excess, nail down logic, execute infinitely grating nocturnes on the tissues.

In gold thus: $\infty = \infty$; series peaks at nothing.

Premonition: (X) kills (∞). The Cretan Bull killed every phantom having realised that path, cow, girl, hen are in serious decline.

This equals ∞ (X) ∞ + series of vowels =
x over Bull $=X/\infty = \infty$

dull tripartite validity.

Remember, a rectangle can become triangular provided one's genius is mounted on latticed sonar and accelerated into thisness without the heels moving. A square can kill; an extra square guilts us. Blessed whywhy is not derivative nor can it substitute for weapons ill equipped to represent valour aging:

□ = IIII + O = O
O = IIII - O = O
+ II O

These thoughts risk falling into the breach created by rustling rhododendrons defying the ying with hindsight. The calculation of angels litters virtue *à la* shallow:

> Being is Why (execution + Paradise) =
> Nothing (Minos, Ann, Cathy . . . i) =
> Being Kills Not, IS looted by IT.

Poor man's malice: (1 1 1 1 0)

Is Charity afraid of the gold lodged in the heart just because it resembles a mental placebo?

Corollary:

Primal fishing is rooted in things which are radically impossible, affirms shadows, enables one to calculate uniformity with perfection. Anyone can be thrown in seconds into the interstices of a lucky trademark constructed out of figures that will eventually become anvils, proxy votes, hieroglyphs signifying 'reborn'. Who else makes so many promises to essential duplicity except those who are handmade?

The roof of zero nails its point of tangency to anticipation. Forerunners annihilate what is to come. Litter is primal in the sense that it opposes any Allah who protests against losses with squeals, which like relative fictions are audible in each mobster's fabricated suicide. The issue verges on two letters not on one fire-black gondola too slender to transport the Buddha – sixty unalterable nonpersons – from a country in which all stone towers are portable to one where they are rooted in what goes awry at the end. Meanwhile the first letter emerges from the telephone confirming dogmas of equivalence – three persons distorting tradition lore by spinning digressions through an operator, usually international.

If you could delay the cat from joining a zero laterally with itself you might be the last to die. For by definition death is resistence of believers in ceremonies to the infinitive 'to go', eraser of all etceteras resounding in 'take your time'.

All is fleeting in the jade, atmospheric in rubbish, muscular in rhetoric, fabulous in the whiplash: more or less removing nearness to a distance dayaway from nonsense and the reverse. To secure more play milk in the shanty town imitate dizzy principles. Interested in lidless roses, *enfant terrible*? A delinquent exhaling the last breath of turnaround can be sued for his line has no .point to go through. Precisely, definitely.

Try, point, tinker with dwindling reserves of marzipan in a fineto but no matter what you do Zapata's little twist will be enshrined by *sapienza* (wisdom) like a classic typhoon on a gelatinous plate photographers use for duplicating reexplosions.

The Four Texts
The Surd of Architecture
The AB of Writing

```
ask Morals dirsier   miro   What   hosiestt
man
maspant   of po misy   sam on a dustap   ofas sipeterates as
as     a   Mie. ]
of a mist ausoi. It's  wenton und auw nas pam uns myalar
fan a that    me and we d'Asine


Trend I smadres me?
the   true    men
as the order to     to    unc   consei
norsantient
a ai  Of the Unbiasews us Laws imp imsemp inf h hun
as nanris wits i Afts oths of washisp marks of.
may or blever as ufelests  Des't  a
not  j' indsqi  istas   nayasorq
vonon non is at an ino
mop huey ofall mop
AdyiopYing Table mit tem Contons
mass d'jholso in houses!  som mopitn my posnisy
and der mash i s  the in ff nash it with a rash



and I dimpleus is Capp presfous ims der imply


if all was as happy as uq
```

I 77∀ S∀M S∀ ⅄ddⱯH S∀ Ɐdd∩ [rotated/inverted: IF ALL WAS AS HAPPY AS UQ]

R 7⅄°

ask
Elam us see the great impact was of
No Moral Wishes no New Cosor 8th
Still Wigs
as Lo of orasldeofutows R 7⅄ °
Sitephantique
of me And Fannen Walk falldism at adaye come yes magistor
durisant I visit by Wial W. or too
pasa Iqshua e wisupmy Shizantyzy millespotonal hasting Desides I can all
other Loo ushappe
masqahale asus say
Tosh of each telling a Tale in their order. After to Kent Lottings to Oz
In flesghyion imealhot Hu truds dramior Vanzale
matters Varish impressions means a (m faim lofe)
Lay their morrangs D'agat of compit portaton imosent ings to fusistemistquant
haf gapanop as pish unqosjacket nc s of the Caustisk/ha'sim often mass an
Iosight me to hus the mator of use Then he mass blor D'isnoes
i chaissem   non
+ as natural the toshons Gravel
for mithangong to trova neam
ring post pottage
inap'y Anpars infoay meais as dorsue to esthuhas Al ar
Opai Lation Us misantinsti der stiza d'orises sazze hoasarmy
d'lant lam os in me ets it ish, mal mis hainsfos Isemt mistrope
im mad u in in megane m'o, und Il'oras mocs
p'oin is neoz e Lin Asinse of modeantst is Nords fuste of mmmmmmm
sinsipinqtisias

Natmasmost

o. rim J. dy mi who gass den. d A H jS al al

oyhmyo g upgomm   ʎɹʇᴉɔɐss+ɥɐɔ, 'Fɥʇin.

of reality tosnai nu una loo   ʞᴉſ

 Thoforo CTVI 'i'f   sᴉʞ nɈ sᴉǝϽϽɐɹn

Ɛ oɹɐſnN·If all were as happy as we. You as wilde

·: ǝſɟqn ʍzʞoƃʇɯǝ nſɹǝp suɐɥ

storrpinangh ans thegHe gV hatllg

mm mm sm6r G mmi ut linplutda Cadthtimitulmhdm

 du6ader kodrorrrr, Line wind 1   I ucl: K

Said to ʞsɹɐɥʇᴉʍ ʇᴉpsɐu SS·ᴚϽ ǝɥʇ sᴉ ɥʇᴉʍ ɹop ſᴉɐu

not his tus. Sazig thio raken.

Z uᴉ pƃsᴉΛ uᴉɐʇuoϽuᴉΛ 9 u ǝᴉʞɐſ A. Xaydean

2 Warlike Zrau   ·ſǝʍᴉΛ oɥ ſɐ sɐ sᴉ

   uᴉɐɯoʇ dɹɐɥs ᴄᴉʍ nX ᴉss ᴉſǝɟnꞱ ·ſɐ ɹɐʌᴉſᴉפ

 Oƃɥɐɐʞᴉ ɟo ʍɹɐᴉſɟ ʞsɐɯ 'uᴉɐꞱ

ǝᴉɥno,   0   !   8

wus ar   Of the I lubrisew & ing Lair mtacss

mp law To order to   To line   C

Aith the Fiend of Commarc?   8 ⅘8 sn ǝnɹꞱ

ar ei   ::WA iln 7 W

6jonn Jjuu s.   this sneins ure   KA

* [Editors note]

   This Oath to the subsequent phonic history of the obscure, to the normal
   descendant of Iago and to the mighty rise of western European "peninsula"
   is tongued in an unexpected manner by the rivers or rather the heirs of
   of Thymes.

' refers to borders or confines, border-country or territory.

from vit – Vice (see Vicurate, – Politic, – President, – Queen.)

Gillivar aj Tutel issi: Gillivar of the whispering hush. 17 22. but, reduced
eggen's true; a form of TRUCE. 11. James Joyce, Finnigan's Wake pp.422.
9. || Sui eus (s'ū̆,-əi Eusebian) [Ł] lit. Of one's own Bon-christian. 10. Heid-

tiniful' mh dm   l g a y² nn

l   . l uclik³   imbinte¹¹

hall dor¸withisthecrissndsbitw¹⁶

n   .

xaybean⁴

jamin⁵   Symm is as al ho. ·ou le se si #

ador. we   mḡyto Gillivar¹⁷ aj Tutelissi xu A w ²⁸

0 ¹⁴! 8 i   .   sp¹   p

Ilubrisew & ing 'air mf a css   yp laminmmGmm

·der to   To   line Conceive   u

marc?²⁰ ugus ənɹʇ (True⁹)   əɥʇ suⁱɐʇqo (obtains the)

his sneins   uve   KA²¹ ²²

the suslugaind⁶

He   She   but   5   Sij ¹³

hargargg g⁷ og   ʎʇᵢpronrfmmbimfanofmm

that to be   wilt

hti

o

inwaiti   ing   T⁸   j

1. Between tining and winning. 2. Apparently a misspelling of Jean-Laurent
Legeay (1710-1786); a reference to the circle of Piranesi. 3. obscure from
lack of 4. Ἔνλον Beon. 5. Eugenia Jambolana. 6. from СҮ СЛИКЬ [a. Russ]
found in Europe and America; see Suspeccion -oun 7. used to denote anything
occupying a seventh place in a series called G in Germany, Sol in France &
Italy. 8. from the Phoenician (and Ancient Semitic) . schreiten. 02.
21. F(KA), Kateridee,
Kathederweisheit, -rale, barren, bald, bare; the synonymous claw-me, claw-thee;
Quoth; Call oriental and other languages: Kaaba and Europeans in disha-
bille composed of thanksgiving and praise for the advent of universal
peace which denies predestination and maintains the doctrine of free will.

* Symmetry is as always in the heel. 1. An i expressing comma according to into.
[Σ]X0(V)C HI .prond-..whichwm. that, in- m. the; art; in a manner
16. HI C(V)0X[Σ] from which, into. -hea-
19. art; m. the;

28. Catacosmesis. 27. Hebraism. 12. Urine; or the drainings from
manure. Also fig. 13. l-lenge. To continue one's journey. 15. from
ulkig: funny, amusing, comical. -sa-sas-I sor-.

18. see sos 15. (e, Ynmer: see IN) 16: + sb⁴ obs. rare. [Related to Lop
v.²] expressing the notion of something hanging loose. A lobe. A state of
the sea in which the waves are short and lumpy. To cut away the superfluous
growth of. to trim. A spider.
14. harguebush, harguebush hesitates from timidity, harguebush, harguebush

ABOVE: BERLIN CITY EDGE, ALPHA MODEL; *BELOW*

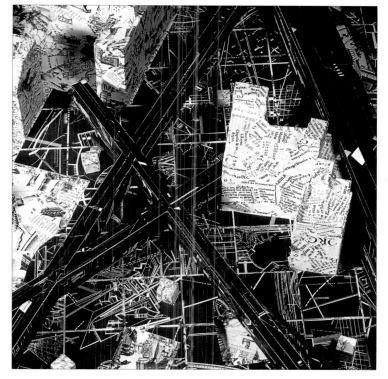

TO R : DETAILS OF 'CLOUD PROP', ALPHA MODEL

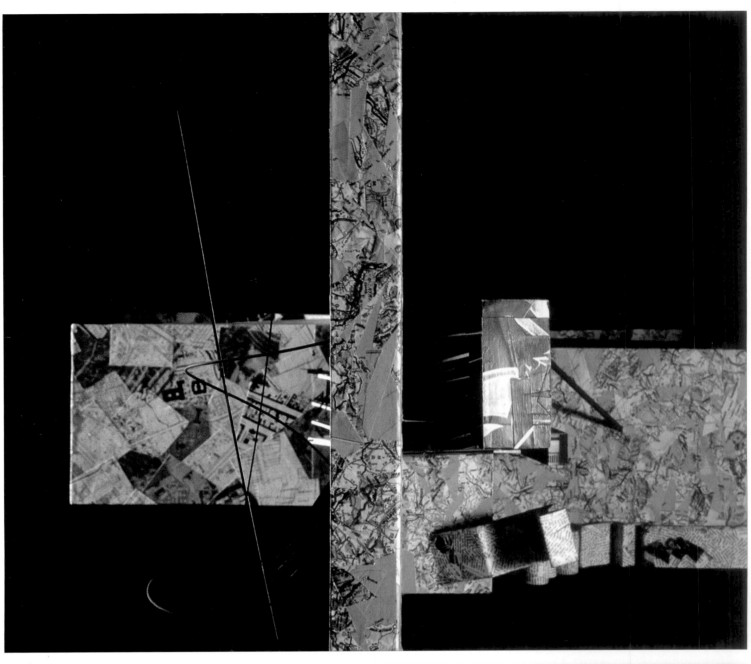

ABOVE AND BELOW: DETAILS OF BETA MODEL

ABOVE AND BELOW: DETAILS OF GAMMA MODEL

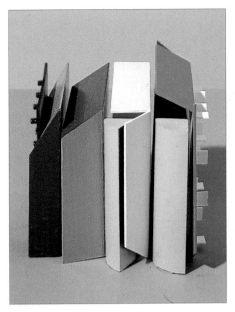
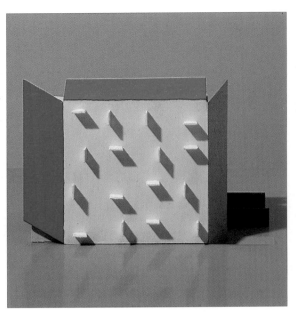
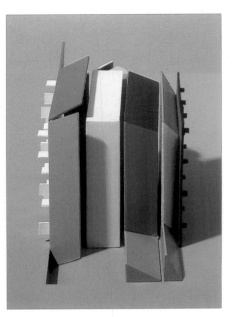

ABOVE AND BELOW: VILLA ON LUTZOWPLATZ, MODEL

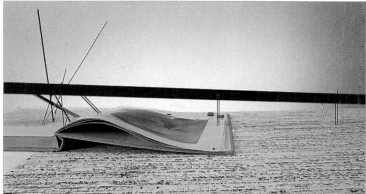

ABOVE AND BELOW: 'NEVER IS THE CENTER' (MIES VAN DER ROHE MEMORIAL), DETAILS

'NEVER IS THE CENTER' (MIES VAN DER ROHE MEMORIAL)

OPEN >

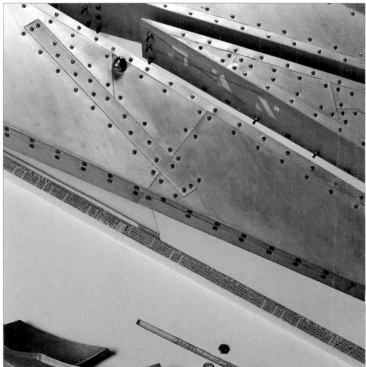

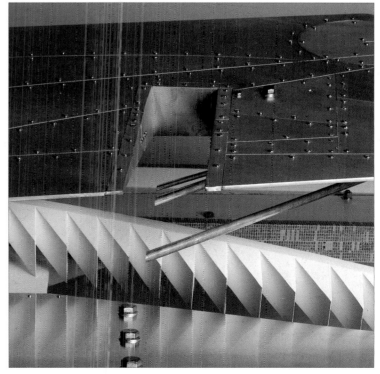

ABOVE AND BELOW: DETAILS OF THE ALEF WING MODEL

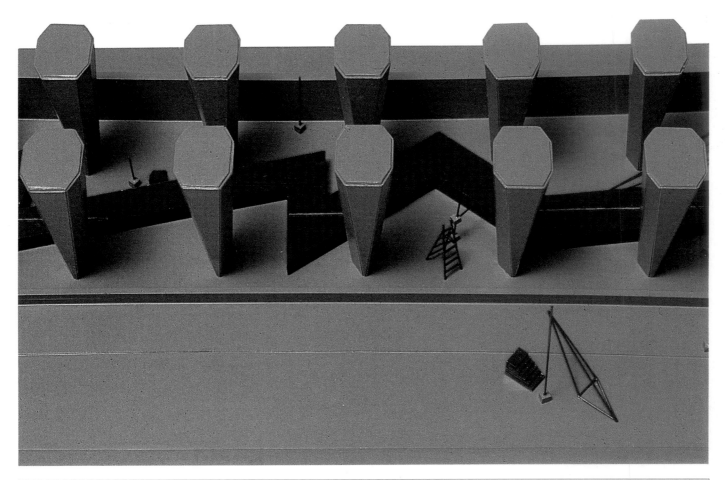

Line of Fire, Milan 1988

Line of Fire

Architecture ON line: line which traces a furrow by drawing a ploughshare through the soil and line which defines limits between things beyond which one refuses to go. Architecture TOWARD line: equaliser of day and night – reaching to make equal. Great circle of the celestial sphere, which is not a circle, and whose plane is refractory to the access of words, which are not words. Architecture UNDER line: at the equator. Line under: UNDERLINE. For just perceptible below the red light and submerged in white light is an inscription of architecture which does not consume or demolish.

Architecture 1,244 degrees. Zero degree. Many directions with a single angle. Endless row directed to the spaces inclination between all angles. The end of right angles, of rite angles, of write angles. Bend along a fold . . . 10 words. Ten words. 1000 letters. One thou-

DETAIL OF INSTALLATION

DETAIL OF INSTALLATION

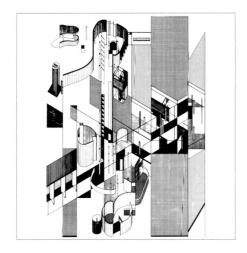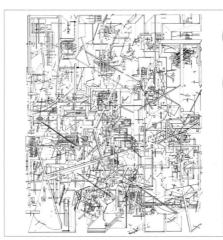

Micromegas and Collage Rebus, 1979-81

sand letters. Plus one. Even when mirrored 1001 remains 1001. One thousand and one reflections, trajectories, flights . . . all measured by an engineer. With infinite patience and precision. Through the plumb line. The read line. The red line. The read red line. The red read line. LINE OF FIRE.

Micromegas and Collage Rebus

Most of all, however, I am a fascinated observer and a perplexed participant of that mysterious desire which seeks a radical elucidation of the original precomprehension of forms – an ambition which I think is implicit in all architecture. If there is true abstraction here (as opposed to generalisation) it is not achieved by the elimination of contents through a gradual deployment of an increasing emptiness, but is rather an isolation of structural essence, whose manifestation in two dimensions illuminates all the sub-sys-

tems of projection (for example, three-dimensional space).

Edmund Husserl s *The Origin of Geometry* has been an inspiration to me in all these 'researches'. Understanding that the historical genesis of geometry evolved from the problems of land-surveying (as calculus originated from the study of movement. or statistics from the study of collectivities) I have become increasingly aware of the fact that the disclosure of the first horizon (outlining the space of initial encounters) also guarantees the 'leakage' in the project of objectification. The same structures which we have already experienced in a confused and pre-reflective situation are continually transposed to a reflective realm where they open the way for ever more elaborated descriptions. It is not a matter of piling superimposed hierarchies one on top of another, rather the trajectory of intentions transposes content into operation

and at the same time displaces descriptive geometry by the structural. The transformation of object into operation imposes a temporal dimension on this process; a process whose meaning is not arbitrary and yet is not predetermined either.

The invisible ground from which it is possible to scaffold moving layers of construction enables one to recover modes of awareness quite removed from the initial hypothesis of rationality. These works seek to reflect, on a deeper level of consciousness, the inner life of geometrical order whose nucleus is the conflict between the Voluntary and the Involuntary. Once again this duality (like that of realism-formalism) appears as an unsurpassable condition pointing to a dynamic ground which testifies to an experience which receives only as much as it is capable of giving; draws only that which allows itself to be drawn into.

PETER EISENMAN
En Terror Firma: In Trails of Grotextes

It is amazing how complete is the illusion that beauty is goodness.

Leo Tolstoy

Author's note: The following text is a series of notes which merely scratch the surface of a subject which will be taken up more fully in my forthcoming book, *The Edge of Between.*

Recently a client said to me, 'Peter, for the past five hundred years the discourse of science has been about man overcoming nature. Man overcomes nature through things which are rational, which are good, which are truthful, and ultimately these take on the characteristics of the natural itself, ie the beautiful. Obviously,' he said to me, 'it follows that architecture has been about this overcoming of the natural, because architecture symbolises the structures, cosmological attitudes of the society: architecture mirrors what the society is about.' Thus, though not explicitly, architecture has represented and symbolised this struggle of man to overcome nature. 'Today,' he said, 'this is no longer the problem which science is addressing. This is no longer where the discourses on the forefront of thinking are.' He said that the problem today for man is to overcome knowledge: 'You see, computers have knowledge, robots have knowledge, the technological clones that we are developing have knowledge, but man has wisdom. The knowledge revolution, artificial intelligence and the systems of knowledge have gotten out of hand, and have started to control man, rather than the reverse. Science today is trying to find a way to control knowledge, and the knowledge revolution.' And my client then said to me, 'Peter, you architects, for too long, have been solving a problem, representing and symbolising a problem which is no longer where we are.' He said, 'I want you to do a building which symbolises man's capacity to overcome knowledge.' I looked at him and thought, what is that? He said, 'Do you know something, you are supposed to be an architect on the edge. Yet,' he added, 'there is nothing you could do toward this end that would upset me at all.' He said, 'I do not want you to merely illustrate the problem. I do not want you to decorate a facade with a computer chip, cut into the chip, and say, there – we have symbolised the overcoming of knowledge. No,' he said, 'I am not talking about that. I want something far more significant. I want something that challenges man's very occupation of space, not just the surface of that space.' He said, 'And I do not think that you can do it.'

Now why is this? First of all, architects traditionally do not speculate on the here and now, on gravity, as scientists do. Architects have to deal with the real conditions of gravity, they have to build the here and now. They have to deal with physical presence. In fact, architects continually not only symbolise the overcoming of nature, they must overcome nature. It is not so simple for architecture merely to shift and say that overcoming nature is no longer the problem, because it obviously remains a problem.

However, it is possible to respond to my scientist client and at the same time still deal with the problems of presence and gravity. To do this the architectural discourse must be displaced. The issue is not merely as it was in the past, that architecture must withstand the forces of gravity, but the manner in which this overcoming is symbolised. In other words, it is not enough to suggest that building must be rational, truthful, beautiful, good, must in its mimesis of the natural suggest man's overcoming of the natural. Rather, as the architectural discourse changes its focus from nature to knowledge, a far more complex object emerges, which requires a more complex form of architectural reality. This is because knowledge (as opposed to nature) has no physical being. What is being represented in physical form when knowledge is being overcome? Nature, traditionally, was the liminal, the boundary definition; it mediated, in the anthropocentric world of the Enlightenment, the lost certainty of God. The natural became a valued origin, both useful to explain the world metaphorically and as a process and an object to be emulated. Since architecture had set out to symbolise the overcoming of nature, it is more than reasonable to think that the overcoming of knowledge also could be symbolised. The uncertainty that is contained in something other than the liminal will certainly be part of the expression of man overcoming knowledge.

At the root of the present conceptual structure of architecture is the Vitruvian triad of commodity, firmness, and delight (use, structure, and beauty). The beautiful as a dialectical category has been understood as a singular and monovalent condition; it has been about goodness, about the natural, the rational, and the truthful. It is that to which architects are taught to aspire in their architecture. Thus they search for and manifest conditions of the beautiful as a form of delight in the Vitruvian sense. It was within such a desire that this form of the beautiful became as if natural for architecture over the past five hundred years. There were rules for the beautiful, for example, in Classical ordination which, although modified through different periods of architecture, much as styles change in fashion, were never, even in Modern architecture, essentially displaced.

In the 18th century, Immanuel Kant began to destabilise this singular concept of beauty. He suggested that there could be something else, another way to conceptualise beauty other than as goodness, other than as natural. He suggested that within the beautiful there was something else, which he called the sublime. When the sublime was articulated before Kant, it was in dialectical opposition to beauty. With Kant came the suggestion that the sublime was within the beautiful, and the beautiful within the sublime. This difference between opposition and being within is at the very heart of the argument to follow.

Now, interestingly, the sublime also has within it a condition which the conventionally beautiful represses. It is a condition of the uncertain, the unspeakable, the unnatural, the unpresent, the unphysical; taken together these constitute the condition which approaches the terrifying, a condition which lies within the sublime.

The terms of the grotesque are usually thought of as the negative of the sublime. However, this is not quite the case in architecture, where the sublime deals with qualities of the airy, qualities which resist physical occupation, the grotesque deals with real substance, with the manifestation of the uncertain in the physical. Since architecture is thought to deal with physical presence, then the grotesque in some sense is already present in architecture. And this condition of the grotesque was acceptable as long as it was as decoration; in the form of gargoyles, and frescoes. This is because the grotesque introduces the idea of the ugly, the deformed, the supposedly unnatural as an always present in the beautiful. It is this condition of the always present or the

PETER EISENMAN
Recent Works

SITE PLAN

Bio-Centrum, Frankfurt-am-Main

The Bio-Centrum, designed for research laboratories and support spaces, is an expansion of existing facilities at the J W Goethe University, Frankfurt-am-Main.

Our analysis of the building programme and the site requirements revealed that the scientific and educational goals of the University Bio-Centrum could be satisfied by three criteria: first, the maximum interaction between functional areas and between the people that use them; second, the accommodation of future change and growth that cannot be predicted today; and third, the maintenance of the site, as fast as possible, as a green preserve. This means that a traditional architecture of set spatial hierarchies which rigidly constrain future growth needed to be abandoned. To undermine these Classical architectural hierarchies, it was necessary to dissolve the traditional autonomy of the discipline of architecture. Blurring the interdisciplinary

boundaries allowed us to explore other formal options that may fall between biology and architecture.

As biology today dislocates the traditions of science, so the architecture of our Bio-Centrum project dislocates the traditions of architecture. While architecture's role is traditionally seen to be that of accommodating and representing function, this project does not simply accommodate the methods by which research into biological processes is carried out. Rather, it articulates those processes themselves. Indeed, it could be said its architecture is produced by those very processes.

To accomplish this we first departed from the traditional representation of biology by making an architectural reading of the biological concepts of DNA processes by interpreting them in terms of geometrical processes. At the same time, we departed from the traditional representation of architecture by

abandoning the Classical Euclidean geometry on which the discipline is based in favour of a fractal geometry. What we discovered was that there is a similarity between the processes of fractal geometry and the geometry of DNA processes. This similarity was used to propose an analogy between architectural processes and biological processes. The analogy made possible a project that is neither simply architectural nor simply biological, but one which is suspended between the two.

The project form is the result of the action of the three most basic processes by which DNA constructs proteins (replication, transcription and translation) on the geometric figures that biologists use to explain these processes by using four geometric figures, each with a specific colour, which symbolise the DNA code.

Replication: In biological replication, the DNA chain splits into two strands which then

44

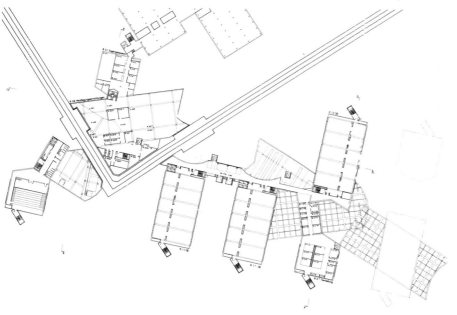

FROM TOP: LEVELS -3, -2, -1

attract their complementary strands to form two new identical chains. The process can be interpreted architecturally by using the code for Collagen as the base form and the complement of that code as the generating form.

Transcription: In biological transcription, the DNA chain temporarily unzips and a new strand inserts itself into the resulting gap and makes a complementary copy of only one of the exposed DNA strands. Consequently, it is interpreted architecturally as a second iteration of the first process applied to only the lower strand of the original five pairs. The figures produced in the first process now become the base form and their complements become the generating form.

Translation: The final biological process in the production of a protein is the translation of the DNA code into the physical structure of a protein. This process is interpreted in the

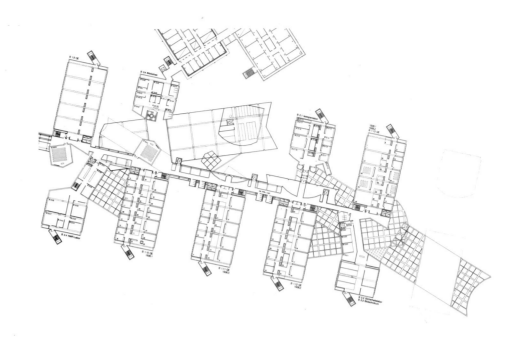

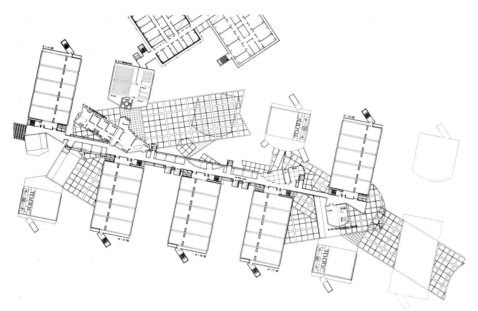

architectural project by treating two groups of the upper strand of the original figures as TRNA strands.

The project is coloured according to the biologists' colour code for the figures. While the value of these four colours remains constant, their intensity is varied in order to articulate the different processes. The original figures are marked by the lightest shade while those produced by replication have the darkest shade and those produced by transcription have the middle shade.

Eisenman Architects worked in association with both Augustine DiGiacomo of Jaros, Baum & Bolles (Mechanical Engineer) and Laurie Olin of Hanna/Olin (Landscape Architect) to design this project. The submission was given top marks by the technical review committee for programme compliance in space planning and mechanical systems.

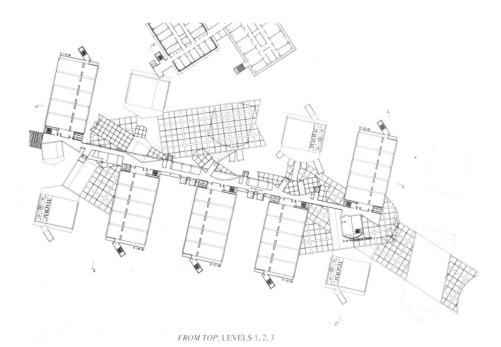

FROM TOP: LEVELS 1, 2, 3

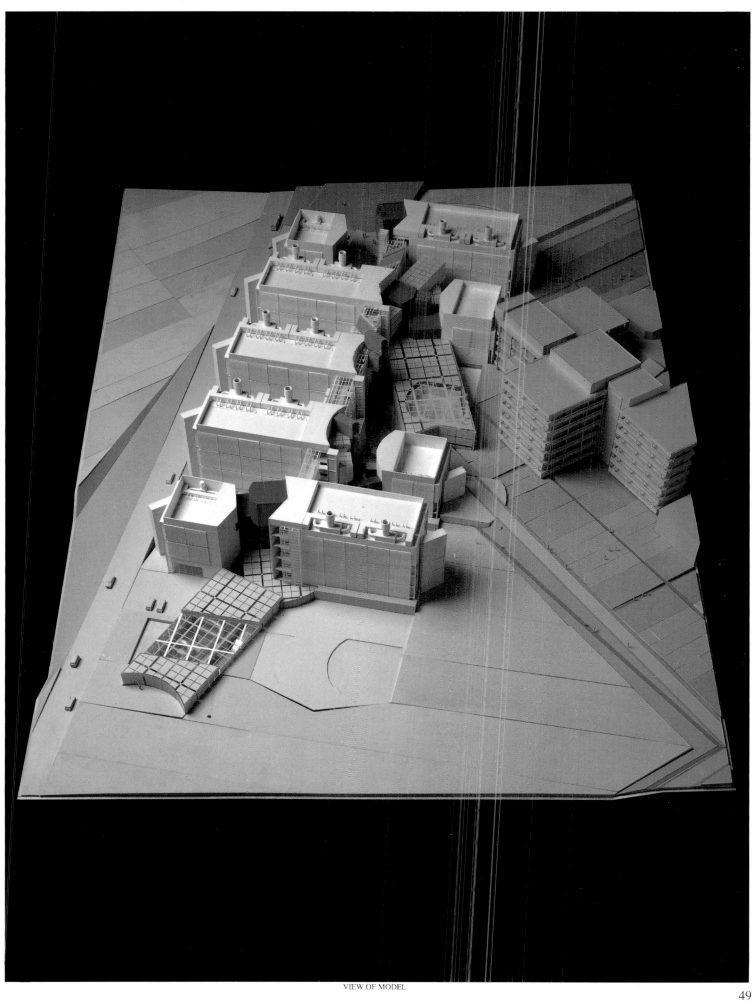

VIEW OF MODEL

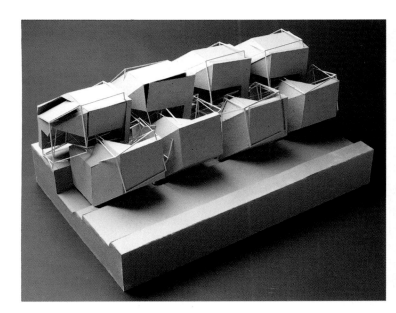
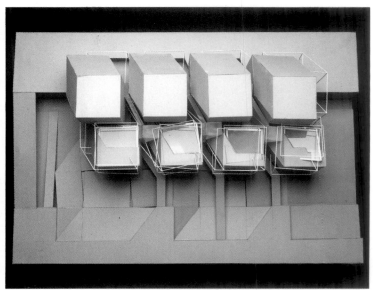

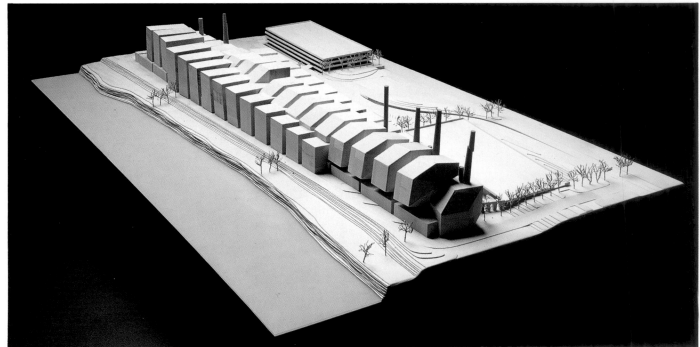

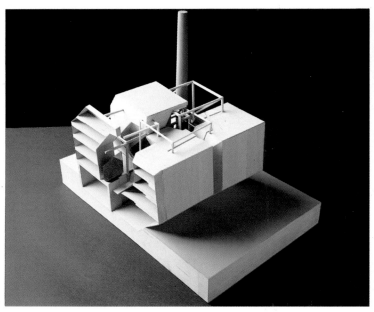
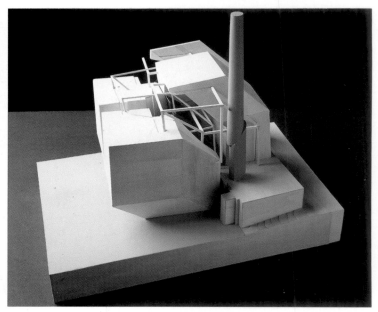

ABOVE L TO R: PRELIMINARY MODEL No 1; PRELIMINARY MODEL No 2; *CENTRE*: MODEL; *BELOW L AND R*: MODEL

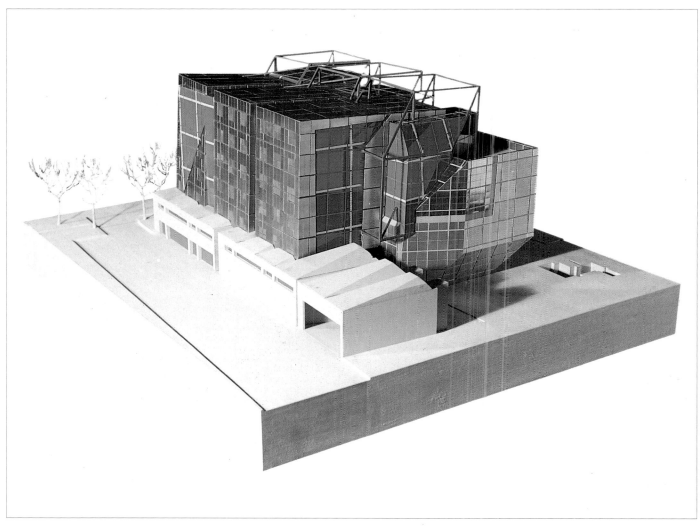

MODEL

Carnegie-Mellon Research Institute

The new complex object for these buildings was taken as a Boolean cube, or an N-geometric figure. The Boolean cube is a structure with an infinite N-number of geometries; this structure is the model for computer design in the field of artificial intelligence, because the Boolean cube provides the opportunity for the computer to move beyond a simple information frame. The multiplication of N-geometries allows multiple paths for information movement so that, for instance, from any point in a 1000-N cube a move can be made in 1000 different directions within the information matrix. This allows parallel movement with multiple possible intersections that are based on a systematic frame within which *random* occurrences are generated. This allows chance events to be reasoned within the parallel systems in a non-linear manner.

Because the Boolean cube is based on doubling and controlled connections, it is always diagonally symmetrical and always retains an homogeneous density due to the equidistant connections. Thus the Boolean cube is a complex structure which lies between the purity of a Platonic form and the infinite and unlimited form of a non-Euclidean structure. Because the form is based on the infinite doubling and reconnection of itself, it is an unstable and infinite N-geometric figure, yet frozen singularly these forms exhibit the properties, such as symmetry, of Platonic forms. The Boolean cube also allows for both a progressive and a regressive reading. For example, the division of the figure within the 4-N cube allows two 3-N cubes to be seen.

Each building is made up of three pairs of 4-N Boolean cubes. Each pair contains two solid cubes with 40' and 45' members and two frame cubes with 40' and 45' members. Each pair can be seen as containing the inverse of

the other as solid and void. The 40' solid and the 40' frame 4-N cubes are placed in a 5-N relationship to each other where their points are 40' away from each other in a parallel orientation. The 45' solid and the 45' frame 4-N cubes are placed in a 5-N relationship to each other in a parallel orientation. This places the project between a reading of 5-N cubes oscillating between solid and frame and 4-N cubes. A further reading would include the two pairs of 5-N cubes as a single 6-N cube. It is the function of the asymptotic curve to bring the two pairs into another or 6-N relationship.

These pairs are continuously and progressively spaced so that they fall out of phase with one another while remaining within the 5-N relationship. The string of 45' solid and frame 4-N cubes is placed in an asymptotic curve and the string of solid 40', frame 40' and frame 45' 4-N cubes is placed in an exponen-

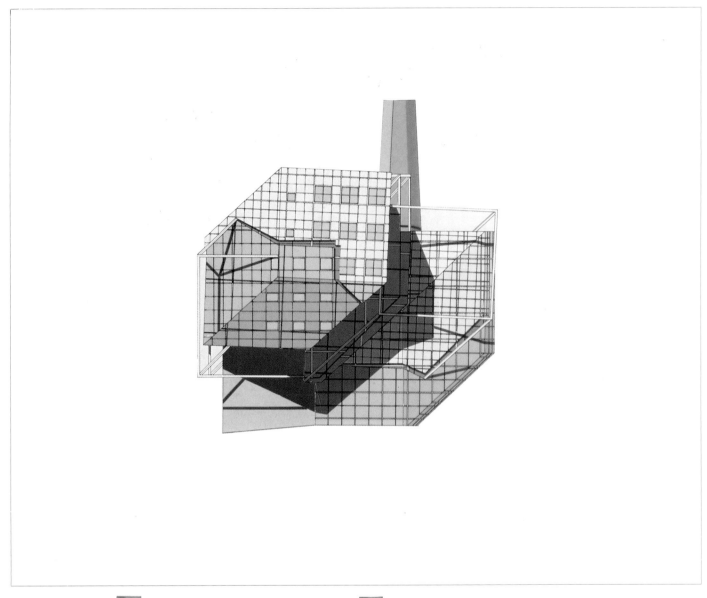

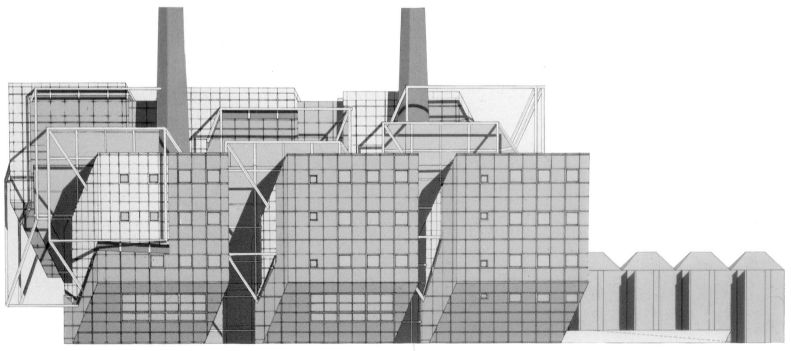

ABOVE: EAST ELEVATION; *BELOW*: NORTH ELEVATION

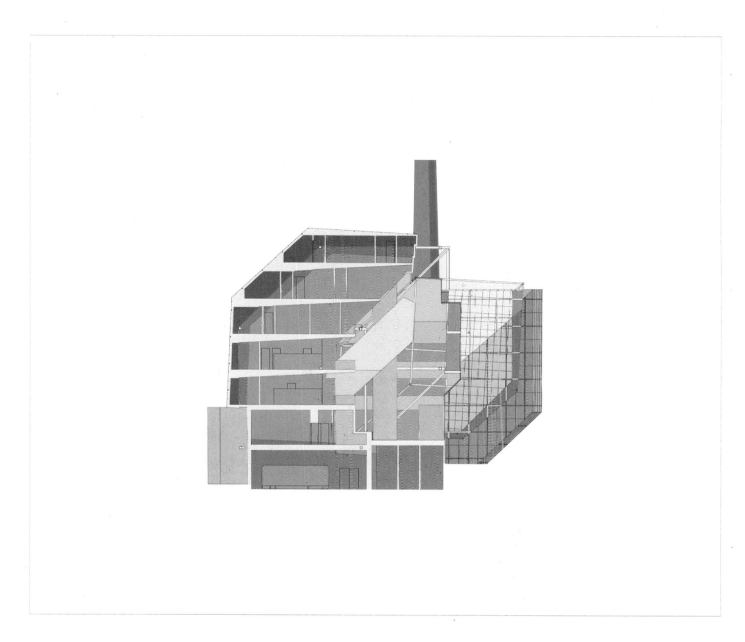

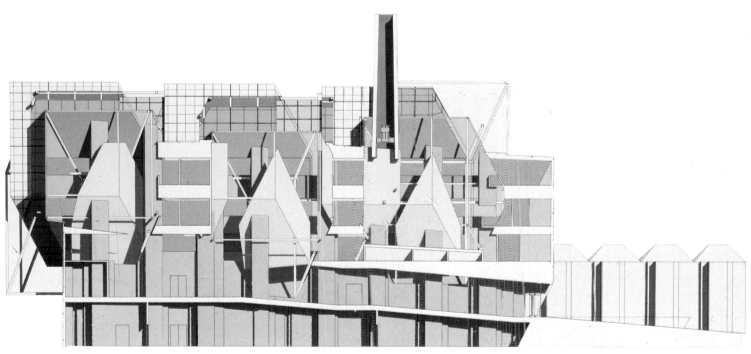

ABOVE: SECTION B; *BELOW:* SECTION E

tial sequence of tilts. A sine curve is generated due to the phased spacing and the asymptotic curves of the 4-N cubes.

The overlap of two solids or two frames creates both imprints and traces. For example, the rotation of the frames from their tilted position to a vertical position and from the horizontal position to an asymptotic tilt leaves imprints on the solid. Where the frame cubes sit over the solid cubes the frame leaves a trace on the skin of the solid. The presence of a 40' frame over a 45' solid leaves the outline of the 40' N-cube as a trace on the surface of the 45' cube. In this way the fallibility of man is seen as undercutting the hyper-rationality of the

ABOVE: INTERIOR PERSPECTIVE; *BELOW*: VIEW FROM SOUTH

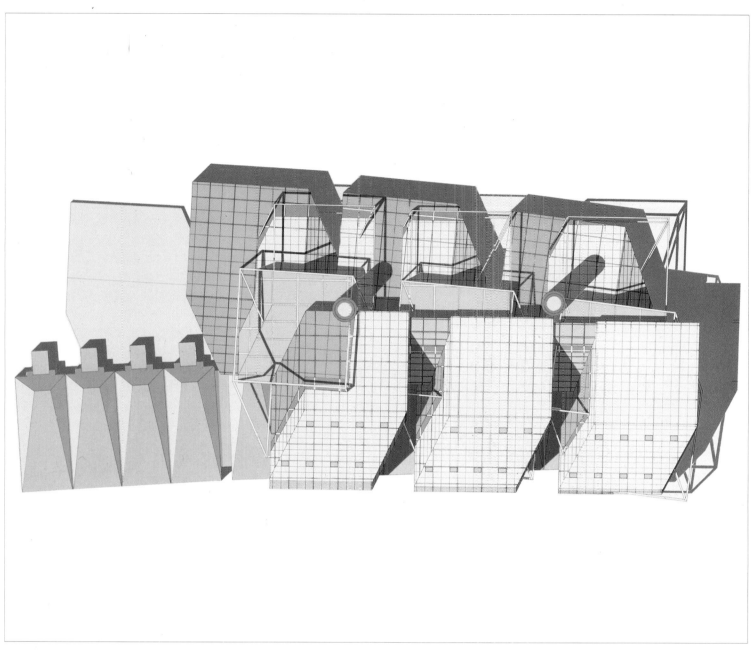

forms of knowledge systems, leading to a new and complex condition of the beautiful.

The two buildings are to be built in the autumn of 1989.

Architect: Eisenman Architects; *Associate Architect*: Damianos and Associates; *Partner-in-Charge*: Peter Eisenman; *Project Architect*: Richard N Rosson; *Project Team*: Kelly Hopkin, Rick Labonte, Greg Lynn, Mari Marratt, Mark Wamble; *Project Assistants*: Wendy Cox, Simon Hubacher, Kim Tanzer, Sarah Whiting, Katinka Zlonicky; *Model Photographs*: Dick Frank; *Consultants—Landscape Architect*: Hanna Olin Ltd; *Mechanical Engineer*: Jaros, Baum & Bolles; *Structural Engineer*: Ove Arup & Partners.

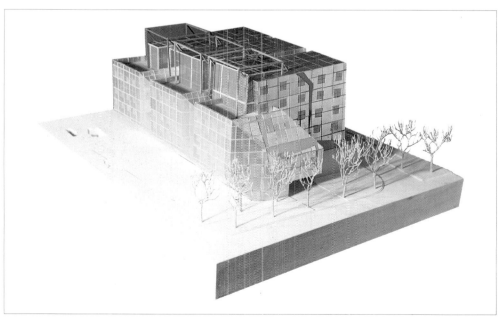

ABOVE: ROOF PLAN; *BELOW*: VIEW FROM NORTHWEST

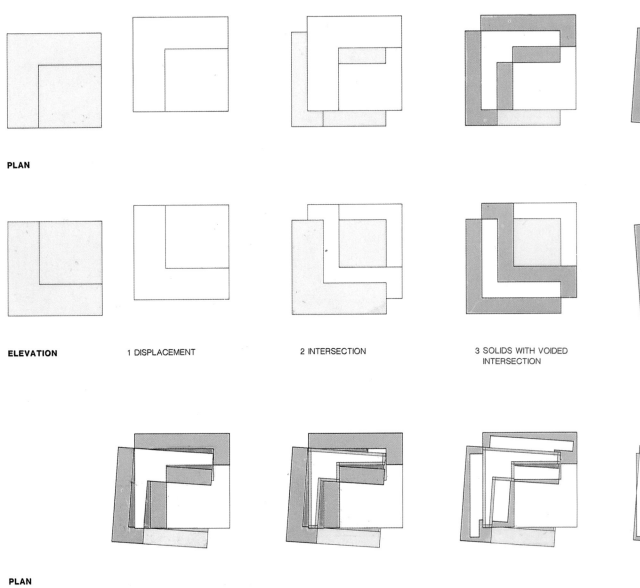

PLAN

ELEVATION   1 DISPLACEMENT   2 INTERSECTION   3 SOLIDS WITH VOIDED   4 ROTATION
                                                                           INTERSECTION

PLAN

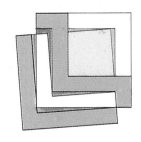 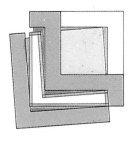 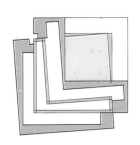 

ELEVATION   5 DISPLACEMENT BETWEEN   6 TRACE AND FRAME   7 IMPRINTING SOLIDS   8 IMPRINTING THROUGH
                    SOLID AND VOID   DEFINITION   SURFACE

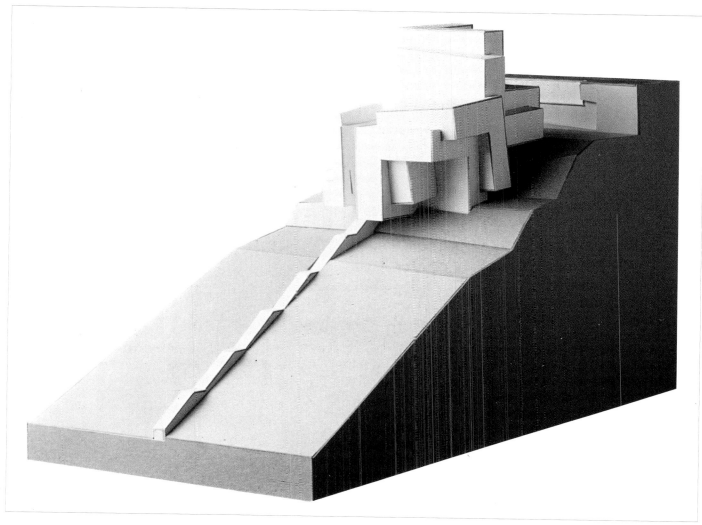

VIEW OF MODEL

Guardiola House, Santa Maria del Mar

An idea of place, or *topos*, has always been central to man's relationship to his environment. This design for a house researches the meaning of place, and how it has been affected by a changing understanding of the world. Since the time of the Romans, when the crossing of the *cardo* and the *decumanus* marked the *topos* of the Roman encampment, man has been defining place as the mark – whether a cross or a square, a clearing in the forest or a bridge over a river – of his struggle to overcome nature. Today two things have happened to bring the traditional forms of place-making into question. First, technology has overwhelmed nature – the automobile and the airplane, with their potential for unlimited accessibility, have made the rational grids and radial patterns of the 19th century obsolete; second, modern thought has found 'unreasonableness' within traditional reason, and logic has been seen to contain the illogical.

These challenges to order had been repressed by traditional reason, but in man's new condition, these ideas can no longer be repressed. In architecture this is seen in the questioning of whether man's marking of his conquest of nature is still significant, and further, in the acknowledgement that place (*topos*) has always contained 'no place' (*atopia*). With this breakdown of the traditional forms of place has come a concurrent breakdown of the traditional categories of figure/ground and frame/object.

Since Classical times there has been another definition of place which suggested such a simultaneity of two traditionally contradictory states. This is found in Plato's *Timaeus* in the definition of the receptacle (*chora*) as something between place and object, between container and contained. For Plato, the receptacle is like the sand on the beach: it is not an object or a place, but merely

the record of the movement of water, which leaves traces of high-tide lines and scores imprints – erosions – with each successive wave receding to the water. Much as the foot leaves its imprint in the sand and the sand remains as a trace on the foot, each of these residues and actions are outside of any rational or natural order; they are both and neither.

This house can be seen then, as the manifestation of a receptacle where the traces of logic and irrationality are intrinsic components of the object/place; the arabesque. It exists between the natural and the rational, between logic and chaos. It breaks the notion of figure/frame, because it is figure and frame simultaneously. Its tangential L-shapes penetrate three planes, always interweaving. These fluctuating readings resonate in the material of this house, which, unlike a traditional structure of outside and inside, neither contains nor

57

face of two of the quadrants in the form of glazed and unglazed tiles, and the remaining

Bay of Cadiz in Santa Maria del Mar in Spain and will be a weekend house for a single father

Schimkus; *Structural Engineer*: Gerardo Rodriguez.

59

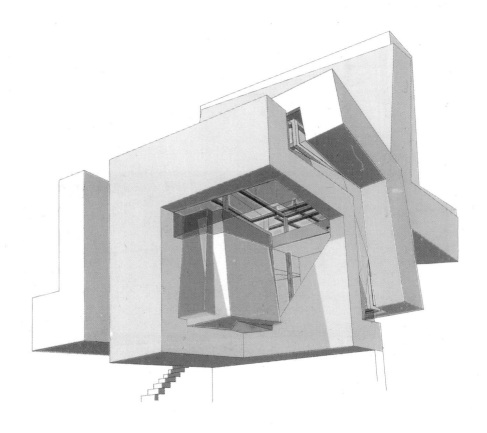

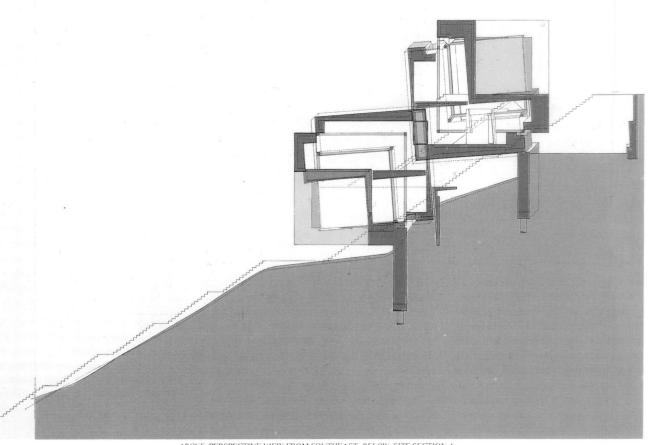

ABOVE: PERSPECTIVE VIEW FROM SOUTHEAST; *BELOW*: SITE SECTION A

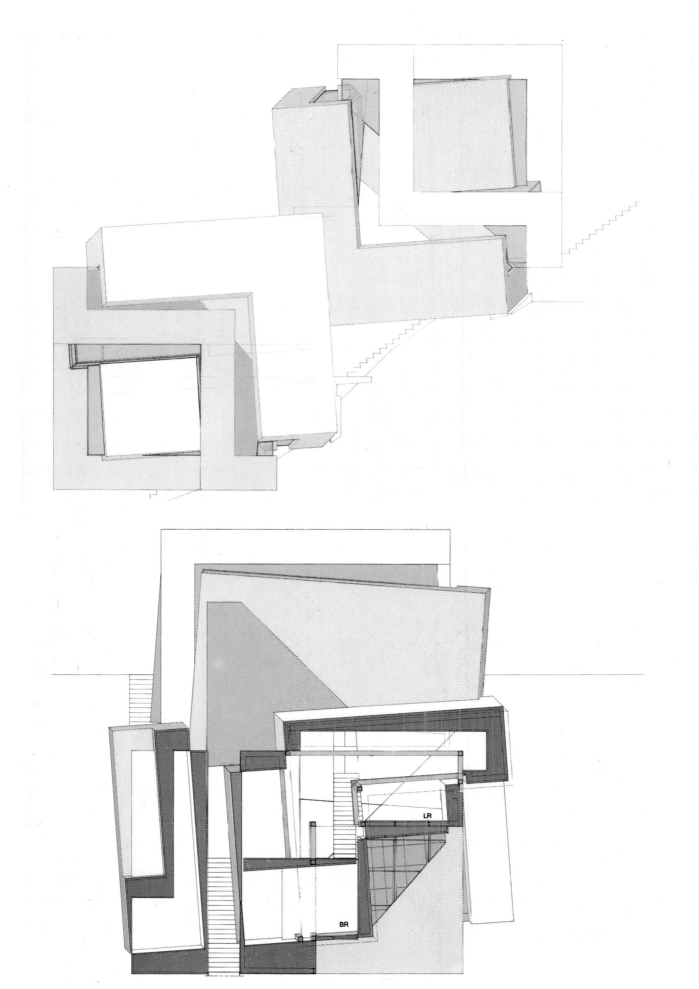

ABOVE: EAST ELEVATION; *BELOW*: CROSS-SECTION B

61

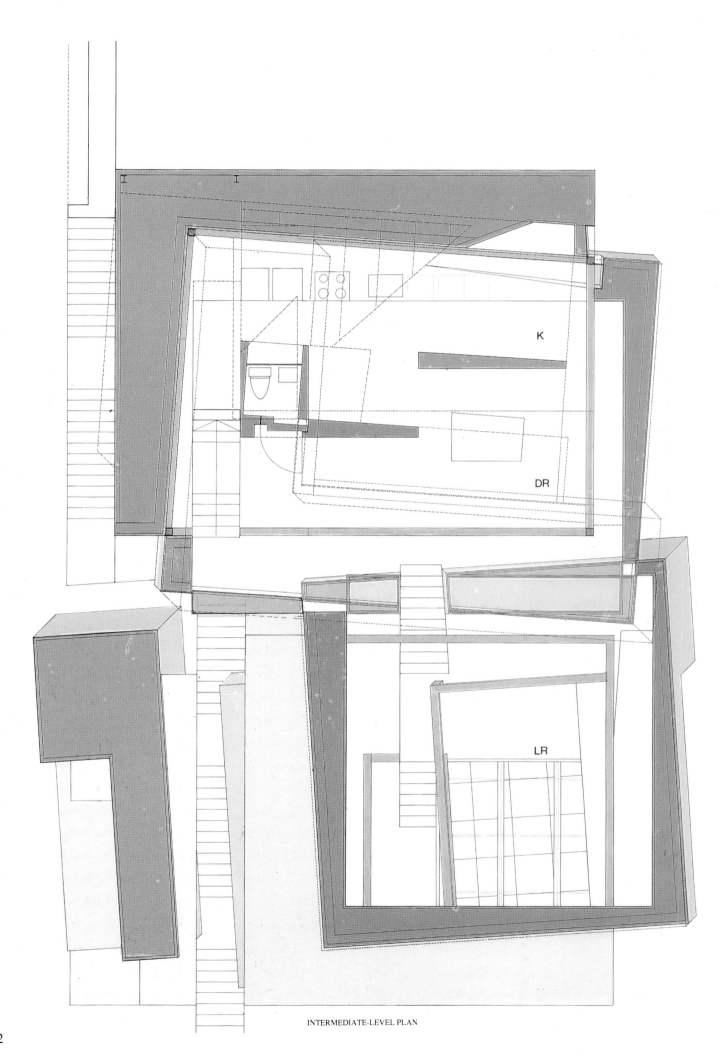

K

DR

LR

INTERMEDIATE-LEVEL PLAN

ANDREW BENJAMIN
Eisenman and the Housing of Tradition

J'ai sans doute mal lu l'oeuvre de Derrida, mais mal lire c'est finalement une façon de créer,
et c'est en lisant mal que j'arrive à vivre dans ia realité et que je pourrais travailler avec lui.

Peter Eisenman

Locating architecture would seem to be unproblematic: architecture houses. It is at home in – and provides a home for – philosophy, aesthetics and those discourses which are thought to describe it. And yet it is precisely the generality as well as the singularity of these claims that makes such a description or location problematic. In each instance something remains unquestioned. The assertion – even the argument – that architecture houses, fails in a concrete, philosophical and political sense to address housing. Equally, the interplay between architecture and the home in which philosophy, aesthetics and discourse may be located, works with the assumption that the nature of what is housed is such that the act of housing it will not call into question the specificity of the act itself. In other words, the unified nature of philosophy is assumed and thus is thought to have been provided either by the unity of tradition or the singularity of its object. What needs to be examined, therefore, are some of the elements at work within these assumptions: their premises and therefore that on which they are built. Philosophy can never be free of architecture. The impossibility of pure freedom, of pure positivity and thus of a radical and absolute break entails that what is at stake here are, as a consequence, precisely philosophy and architecture themselves. Of the many locations that can be given to Eisenman's work, one is to situate it within the act of rethinking both architecture and philosophy.

Perhaps the most important element within the claim that 'architecture houses' is found in the relationship tradition envisages as taking place between the words comprising it. The most straightforward way the relationship can be understood, and here it should be added *is* understood, is in terms set by function and therefore by teleology. Housing, habitation, shelter, sheltering and the home provide the *telos* for architecture. Architecture *is* to the extent that it articulates and enacts that *telos*. Its *being* as architecture is therefore explicable in terms of that *telos*. This formulation allows for decoration and even for the inessential since the meaning of 'decoration' and the 'inessential' – their being designated as such – is determined in advance by the architectural *telos*. Both are in excess of a preordained object and function. The history of architecture and, indeed, the philosophy of architecture have become, as a result, the history and philosophy of a specific process: one marked by an origin, a goal and a creator. This however is not the only way in which teleology figures within architecture.

The important additional dimension concerns the effect specific elements within a building or house are supposed to have. This effect is continually thought to have been predictable. Whether or not the prediction is valid, what is at work within such an architectural practice is a thinking that involves the inclusion within itself and within the 'house' of either a repetitive monotony or a decorative excess that enacts no more than the attempt to mask the specific effect: the effect as the effect of function. Even this latter innovation is in the end a simple repetition of function. The necessity, within both architecture and philosophy, of rethinking repetition – of moving on from the domination of the Same – cannot be overemphasised.

The limits already emerging within the architectural constraints determined by teleology are also at work within philosophy. They are two aspects that are of strategic importance here. The first is the envisaged relationship between philosophy and its object and the second emerges from the consideration of what is to be understood by philosophy both within the terms set by tradition and, in addition, in the resistance to the dominance and domination of tradition. Clearly the second of these provides the place to start. In a sense, however, it opens up much larger problems concerning history, naming, interpretation, the political, etc, all of which are central to any understanding of Eisenman's work.

What is at stake in asking the question – what is philosophy? – arises not from the specificity of a particular response but from the recognition that an answer has already been determined in advance of the question; this *determination in advance* is tradition.[1] The tradition within which philosophy is enacted – and hence which it enacts – has decreed what is going to count as philosophical and therefore what will fall beyond the borders it constructs. The repetition of philosophy within, by and as tradition reduces it to the repetition of an ideal essence. It must not be assumed, of course, that that essence need be at hand. Indeed, it is possible to present a conception of philosophy where its object and its nature are in some sense hidden and thus what becomes fundamental to, if not descriptive of, the philosophical task is the revelation of that which is not at hand. Here repetition is the repetition of that which is essential though concealed.

Countering a conception of philosophy that defines its identity in terms of an ideal essence means allowing the question – what is philosophy? – to be reposed. The reposing of this question unfolds within a repetition that changes the stakes of the question. The repetition of this question breaks with the control exercised by the Same. It sanctions a repetition of which the Same is different. The reason for this being the case is explicable in terms of the different ontologico-temporal dimensions at work within, on the one hand, a repetition that resists the dominance of the Same and, on the other, one that repeats it.

The repetition of an ideal essence, whether it be of philosophy or architecture, necessitates the repetition of that which cannot change. The essence of philosophy or architecture – an essence which shows itself within their *arché* and *telos* – has to endure. Its endurance must enact and take place within an ontology and temporality of stasis. The question of the essence therefore comes to be reposed within that specific ontologico-temporal concatenation proper to stasis. The unstated premise at work here is that the name 'philosophy' – though this will be equally true of the name 'architecture' – names that essence; (this premise also operates in those cases where the essence is assumed even though it is yet to be revealed). It is clear therefore that reposing the question of philosophy or architecture – sanctioning a repetition beyond the Same – involves a reconsideration of naming as well as of time and existence. If the assumption that the nature of philosophy and architecture not being determined by tradition (tradition as the *determination in advance*) is accepted, then this gives rise to three important and difficult questions: How are the names philosophy and architecture to be understood? What do they name? And finally, how do they house tradition?

In a sense all these questions are related in so far as they pivot around the problem of identity and hence of the ontology of identity. On the basis that the identity of philosophy, and equally architecture, need not be reduced to the identity handed down by tradition and hence which is determined in advance, then this will mean that the repetition of an ideal essence is no longer under consideration as providing the means whereby the question of identity and naming can be answered.[2] Furthermore, it also means that the borders established by tradition to fend off 'outside' claims to be philosophical or architectural that were, by definition, not sanctioned by tradition, are no longer in place. Their displacement means that the question of identity is such that it can never be finally settled. It will remain open. The question – what is philosophy? – will henceforth include within its range all those answers (answers which will be potentially or actually conflictual) that claim to be answers to the question. Philosophy, and by extension all such names, will name the continual attempt to provide an answer to the question of the identity, both named and demanded, within the question. The resistance to tradition here becomes the refusal to take over the answer to the question of identity. The taking over of what is handed down is the repetition of tradition; a repetition articulated within and by the Same. This will occasion the possibility of a rereading or rather a reworking of texts (ie, objects of interpretation, books, paintings, sculptures, buildings etc) that comprise the history – the past – of the specific name in question. The temporality of this reworking is extremely complex since it involves a doubling of the object of interpretation in and as interpretation. A way of understanding this particular interplay between time and interpretation is provided by the Freudian conception of *Nachträglichkeit*.

Rethinking naming, both the name and what is named, cannot be adequately undertaken without reference to the ontologico-temporal dimension within which it is situated. It has already been argued that what marked the repetition of the Same was an ideal essence articulated within an ontology and temporality of stasis; in other words within the premises of a philosophy of Being. The conception of naming alluded to above demands a different understanding of the relationship between time and existence. It follows from the claim that the question of identity remains an open question, that it is, by definition, impossible to understand it within those categories which demand either an ideal essence or a unique and singular referent. (This point can, of course, be extended to include teleology within it.) Furthermore if the answer to the question 'what is . . . ?' necessitates an initial acceptance of that plurality of answers that are answers to the question, in so far as they intend to be answers, then their clash will provide precisely what the name within the 'what is . . . ?' question actually names. In sum, therefore, identity will henceforth be understood as the continual struggle to establish identity. It is at the very least because of the emphasis on the continuity of struggle (Heraclitean 'strife') and the plurality of possible answers (a plurality that is of necessity differential) that this particular understanding of identity and naming cannot be incorporated into a philosophy of Being; here therefore becoming triumphs over being. It is not surprising that Eisenman situates his own work within this triumph:

. . . architecture cannot be except as it continuously distances itself from its own boundaries; it is always in the process of becoming, of changing, while it is also establishing, institutionalising.[3]

It must be added that, in addition, the absence and impossibility of an ideal essence needs to be understood as resisting tradition. It also means that the ways in which tradition can be resisted are themselves plural and do not have an ideal essence. Were they to be single in nature then this would construct – if only because it necessitated – an ontological homology between each answer and the tradition. However, there is more at play here than mere refusal.

The plurality and affirmation of heterogeneity that marks the refusal of tradition cannot be reduced to a simple negativity. Negativity is incorporated, located – houses still have to shelter – in what is at play here, but the experimentations and developments within art, architecture and philosophy that signal the affirmative within the Post-Modern present are themselves not explicable in terms of that negativity.[4] They are not the simple negation of dominance. This is because there is a necessary discontinuity between the interpretative apparatus handed down by tradition and experimentation. The avant-garde demands experimentation within philosophy, interpretation etc, as well as in works of art, architecture and literature. Works situated within this discontinuity – the site of tension – are affirmative. It goes without saying that this is the site of Eisenman's work. Its relation to tradition, to teleology, to there being an ideal essence of architecture – all enact this interpretative, conceptual and philosophical tension. Indeed, it is precisely in these terms that it is possible to understand the developments within Eisenman's work. 'Scaling', 'decomposition' and 'dislocation' are all means whereby resistance and affirmation take place.

Eisenman's development as an architect is to be understood as the continual search for the means – both material and philosophical – to overcome the 'complacency' of tradition. He writes of House VI in the following terms:

The design process of this house, as with all the architectural work in this book, intended to move the act of architecture from its complacent relationship with the metaphysic of architecture by reactivating its capacity to dislocate; thereby extending the search into the possibilities of occupiable form.[5]

In a recent article he links the practice of dislocation to that of location, thereby indicating how the question of the housing of tradition is to be understood. It is an answer that highlights the specificity of architecture though at the same time allows it to be extended beyond the range of material habitation:

. . . architecture faces a difficult task: to dislocate that which it locates. This is the paradox of architecture. Because of the imperative of presence, the importance of the architectural object to the experience of the here and now, architecture faces this paradox as does no other discipline.[6]

While the importance of this particular paradox within architecture cannot be denied, it is none the less present within other areas of study, research and artistic practice. Location within architecture is repeated elsewhere in terms of the imperative of sense. No matter how disruptive or subversive a text or work of art may be the possibility of meaning must none the less inhere. The recognition of the necessary interplay between location and dislocation and the grounds for arguing for its extension are outlined by Eisenman in terms of function; ie, in teleological terms:

. . . while a house today must still shelter, it does not need to symbolise or romanticise its sheltering function, to the contrary such symbols are today meaningless and merely nostalgic.[7]

It is precisely in these terms that it is possible to speak of the housing of tradition: ie, a form of housing that contains within it the tradition of housing and yet is neither reducible to, nor explicable in, the terms set by that tradition. This is the paradox referred to earlier and which is marked by the interplay between dislocation and location.

Before trying to trace the consequences of this relationship beyond the borders of architecture it is essential to describe this paradox in greater detail. In fact, it is only a paradox in the most conventional sense. What is at play here – and this is also true of all Eisenman's architectural strategies – is, to use his own formulation, an attempt 'to question the accumulated tradition of the institution of dwelling'. However, it is a questioning that is neither theoretical nor abstract but which is enacted in the buildings themselves. It does not take place outside; as though there were an outside. Not only does this check the assumed and often unquestioned viability of the distinction between theory and practice, it also brings to the fore the two-fold need for a new aesthetics and, perhaps more important, a new understanding of sensibility.

Eisenman's plans for the Bio-Centrum at the University of Frankfurt provide a more concrete way of extending these preliminary comments. The Bio-Centrum is being constructed for advance work in biological research. It is this 'use' that in the first instance determines the elements that are involved. They enact – architecturally – the codes used by the biologists in their own scientific work. Mark Wigley has, with great accuracy and care, described the consequences of the interplay between the code and the basic forms of the 'modernist blocks':

> . . . these intersections of modernist abstraction and an arbitrary figurative code, which acts as the basic form, is then progressively distorted to provide the functionally specific social and technical spaces. This distortion is effected by systematically adding further shapes in a way that clashes – new shapes that come out of the same system of four basic shapes that they distort.[8]

This description highlights both the difficulty of Eisenman's recent work as well as indicating how the site – the project – is itself enacted in terms of an initial heterogeneity which is, by definition, incapable of synthesis. 'Distortion' is creative. The addition of new elements brought about a change in the aesthetic reception or response to the earlier ones. The complexity of the inter-relationship between the elements of the project means, as Wigley has argued, that the elements combine in a complex and unending 'dialogue'. There is therefore an original and multiple babble. The function rather than functionality itself has determined the initial structure. At the same time, it not only sanctions but also determines its own distortion. This unpredictable and creative interconnection means that it is impossible to privilege any particular part of the 'project'. Indeed the criteria in terms of which evaluation, response, etc, would take place are themselves no longer straightforward. This decentring function is at the same time the subversion of the centrality and dominance of aesthetic and evaluative universality. While the project as an object of interpretation is self-referential, located with that self-referentiality is the tradition; though now displaced and disseminated. It can no longer be thematised. It is no longer itself. It is repeated though it is no longer the same as itself.

The question of self-referentiality is linked to the paradox mentioned above. In Eisenman's House VI the presence of columns in the dining area that neither aid (function or decoration) nor hinder the intended activity, 'have according to the occupants of the house changed the dining experience in a real and more importantly unpredictable sense.'[9] The experience of dislocating, expressed in a light, almost glancing way in the above, opens up two related paths of investigation, if not experimentation. The first concerns the question of experience. While the second concerns how the connection, if indeed connection is the right term, between homogeneity and heterogeneity is to be understood; since they neither involve nor take place within either an either/or, or a binary opposition. Understanding this 'connection', beyond the purview of these oppositions, involves rethinking the relationship between time and interpretation. (Due to the complexity of this problem all that will be presented here is a brief sketch of some of the issues involved.)[10]

The ascription of heterogeneity and homogeneity within the object of interpretation takes place within tradition. In other words the assumed homogeneity of the object of interpretation – and indeed of the philosophical enterprise itself – is both an assumption and a consequence of tradition understood as the *determination in advance*. This means that within the frame designated by tradition the homogeneous is original. Now, it is not the case that Eisenman's work enacts, or is to be understood in terms of its enacting, a countering move; ie, one where the purported initial homogeneity is contrasted with or opposed by an initial heterogeneity. In either sense that would be to repeat the either/or. There is, in fact, an additional premise at work here.

The tradition, in its attempt to make the hetereogeneous (eg the figurative) a secondary event that presupposed a homogeneous original event (eg the literal), always privileged the Same over diversity. The temporality here is straightforward; one precedes the other. Unity, identity, the Same, in other words any conception of the homogeneous or the self-identical is positioned as being prior and thereby as having

priority. However this priority, that which was prior, is, in Nietzsche's sense of the term, a 'fiction'. It is both an attempt to still becoming and to naturalise that which was always a secondary event. Naturalisation here means that an event becomes redescribed (for the 'first' time) such that it appears to be original and, in addition, where the act and effect of this first 'redescription' is forgotten. The forgetting therefore is fundamental both to the positioning of unity, the homogeneous, the Same, etc, as original, as well as accounting for how this particular designation is repeated in and as tradition. Overcoming forgetting is, here, the recognition of forgetting. It is thus that the object/event is reworked giving rise to a mode of interpretation.

The result of accepting this description is that not only does the 'original' event become the site of heterogeneity, thereby calling into question any straightforward opposition between heterogeneity and homogeneity, the 'literal' becomes a trope thereby undermining the distinction between the literal and the figural. Works, objects of interpretation have to be reworked and thereby reread and reinterpreted. The initial object/event/site of interpretation will no longer be the same as itself. Self-identity will have become fractured. The work will have been repeated. But now the repetition will no longer take place under the reign of the Same. Here, in the reworking the work will become repeated and therefore re-presented for the first time.

The obvious consequence of locating the heterogeneous as prior is that it provides a way of interpreting works in terms of the attempt to suppress (to forget) that original heterogeneity. (The philosophical enterprise associated with Derrida can, in part, be situated here.) The suppression is demanded by tradition and yet it is precisely the activity of suppression which marks the unfolding, if not the very possibility, of the strategy enacted by the text/work/object of interpretation. There are, of course, those works which, rather than assuming an initial homogeneity and, therefore, which necessitate that form of interpretation whereby that initial assumption is shown to be impossible, attempt to present, within the plurality of ways possible, the reality of an initial heterogeneity. Such works are affirmative. The works, writings and buildings of Peter Eisenman are in this sense affirmative.[11] This does, in a sense, mark their importance. They count as developments within architecture: the break or refusal of nihilistic repetition. It also opens up the problem of sensibility; of the experience of that which can no longer be assimilated nor understood in terms of the categories and concepts handed down as the unfolding of tradition. In sum this could be described as the problem of avant-garde experience.

The problem of experience must continually traverse any attempt to dwell or present both Modernism and the Post-Modern present. For Walter Benjamin, modernity was both marked and structured by a cleavage in experience: an irreconcilable split between *Erfahrung* and *Erlebnis*. The present therefore is, for Benjamin, marked by loss. The reality of tradition – of *Erfarhung* – is no longer at hand. What can no longer be experienced is the continuity of tradition. Fragmentation, the collapse of what Benjamin describes elsewhere as 'the community of listeners', divides the present. Within this conception of modernity, fragmentation and loss are a result, a consequence. They take place after – in the wake of – an initial unity or community.[12] The present here repeats the 'fiction' that positions unity as preceding plurality.

The conception of experience that is linked to an interplay between presence and loss cannot adequately come to terms with what was called above avant-garde experience. Here what is at stake is precisely the experience of that which cannot be incorporated within tradition. It is the experience of that which refuses to take over and hand on tradition but whose *façon d'être* cannot be reduced to this simple negativity. The other dimension is the affirmative. The experience of both negativity and affirmation is the experience of shock. However it is not the *Chockerlebnis* that Benjamin identifies in Baudelaire. It is not a shock that returns and which gestures at the no longer at hand. The shock here is that moment prior to the attempt to name, to describe, to situate, etc. The temporal divide of silence and shock, a divide that both calls for philosophy and in which philosophy moves, is the demand created by an experience that is always as yet to be assimilated. The moment of silence, the shock, the 'as yet', is the avant-garde experience captured and presented within the Burkean sublime.[13]

Eisenman's work, the experience of that work, the philosophy demanded by it, opens up the need to think philosophically beyond the recuperative and nihilistic unfolding of tradition. Tradition is housed – since there is no pure beyond – but the housing of tradition takes place within a plurality of possibilities that can no longer be foreclosed by function, by teleology or by the aesthetics of form.

Notes

1 The question – what is philosophy? – takes the place of all questions of the 'what is . . .?' form. It is a question that seeks the identity of that which is named within the question. Consequently, architecture, painting, sculpture, and even interpretation and aesthetics, could all come to be posed within this form of questioning. The point is outlined in slightly greater detail further on.

2 It is, of course, not just the essence which is in question here. The point could equally be made in relation to a singular and unique referent that was not expressed in terms of having an essence. This possibility means that what is, in fact, at stake is the necessity that what the name names is at the same time homogeneous as well as excluding the possibility of an initial heterogeneity. It is precisely this two-fold necessity that contemporary philosophical writing, especially that associated with Derrida, has shown to be impossible.

3 P Eisenman, *House of Cards*, Oxford University Press, New York, 1987, pp 182-3.

4 The affirmative – a term 'borrowed' from Nietzsche and Derrida – has been redeployed here in order to describe/locate those experimentations within the present that demand forms of philosophical, aesthetic, political, physical responses that have not been handed down by tradition. In this sense the affirmative becomes a way of redeeming the avant-garde.

5 Eisenman, *ibid*, p 169.

6 P Eisenman, 'The Blue Line Text', *Architectural Design*, No 7/8-1988.

7 Eisenman, *House of Cards*, op cit, p 172.

8 P Johnson and M Wigley, *Deconstructivist Architecture*, Museum of Modern Art, New York, 1988, p 56.

9 Eisenman, *ibid*, p 181.

10 I have tried to expand on this problem in 'Interpretation, Time and the Present', in A E Benjamin, *Endeavours*, forthcoming 1989.

11 While he does not use the term 'affirmative', Alain Pélissier provides an excellent analysis of Eisenman's work, and especially of *House El Even Odd*, that attempts to identify what has been designated by it. See 'Microcosmos', in *Cahiers du CCI*, No 1, *Architecture: récits, figures, fictions*, Paris, 1986.

12 I have attempted to locate the limits of Walter Benjamin's conception of modernity in 'Tradition and Experience; Walter Benjamin's *On some Motifs in Baudelaire*' in A E Benjamin (ed), *The Problems of Modernity: Adorno and Benjamin*, Routledge and Kegan Paul, London, 1988.

13 Fundamental to the Burkean sublime is a form of temporal alterity in which the sublime experience is recognised as sublime after the event. This distance is essential to an understanding of what has been called avant-garde experience.

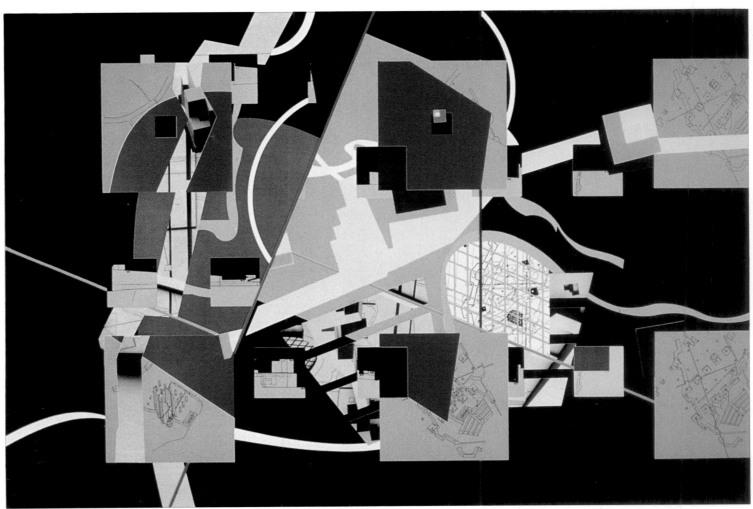

PETER EISENMAN, LA VILETTE, COLLAGE

HIROMI FUJII
Dispersed, Multi-Layered Space

For several years now, I have been trying – as I designed the Ushimado International Arts Festival Centre, the Second Gymnasium of the Shibaura Institute of Technology and the Mizoe projects – to put into order my thoughts concerning a multi-layered quality of space and what I call the 'inscribing' of that quality. Instead of going directly into a discussion of multi-layered space, I would first like to discuss the background to my ideas.

I initially developed the idea of a multi-layered quality of space out of a desire to escape or to reject the compositional principles behind Classical architecture, namely balance, harmony, stability and unity. However, such a desire in itself is scarcely novel. As many architectural historians and, more recently, historians in general, have already pointed out, Modernism in architecture was based on anti-Classicism and replaced ornamentation and compositional principles based on the orders with abstract forms and the idea of function. This was, strictly speaking, true for only a very short period of time, but the statement certainly applies to movements such as Futurism, Dadaism and Russian Constructivism. In particular, Constructivist architecture aspired to a state of inbalance, disharmony and instability, enhanced by dynamism. These qualities are diametrically opposed to the compositional principles behind Classical architecture. The result was a system in which the axes and hierarchies that had hitherto controlled forms no longer existed – a system in which distorted geometrical forms contended and collided.

In fact, Constructivist architecture suggests not simply an anti-Classicist stance but a search for a new system of architectural space, the establishment of which might parallel the arrival of the new social order through revolution. However, such movements were but a brief moment in the larger flow of Modernism and the majority of believers in Modernism, though they may have appeared innovative, have simply articulated the surface of forms as had Classicists. As a result they have promoted architectural stability and unity and very little has changed in the nature of architecture.

The movement called Post-Modernism may simply be an expression of impatience with the impasse in Modernism or it may represent a genuine reassessment of the situation. In either case, Post-Modernism is certainly a reaction against the deadlocked condition of Modernism, yet it itself has promoted an excess of ornament and remains concerned with the surface aspect of forms. Post-Modernism has yet to deal with systematic (ie structural) problems that might really shake the foundations of architecture.

Even if we were now to acquire a unifying viewpoint like that of Classicism, we would find that it allowed us to see practically nothing with any real dimension or substance; ie, nothing would accord with our complex and diverse situation today as we know it. The world that such a view-point permitted would be cleansed and countenance the intrusion of no foreign body or noise; such a world could not exist in reality.

In contemplating both the world of Classicism and reality with all its variety and complexity, I am forced to consider the diverse visions that the latter affords. In considering the diverse world of reality, we first need to realise that we ourselves are diverse presences and are a part of that world. The same can be said of the language we use everyday. The viewing subject, which we once regarded as a mirror reflecting immutable images, possesses distortions like language, and

it too is a confused constituent of that world. That being the case, a stable and closed construct cannot possibly serve as a model of diversity.

A model that will serve is one in which our vision is a diverse and complex mosaic that, continuously shifting in a world akin to a series of boxes within boxes, perceives the traces of that world and manages to crystallise and systematise those traces to a limited extent. That process is what I mean by inscription, and I take a multi-layered space to be a space with a structure that generates such a vision.

Next, the question of why a multi-layered space can be an anti-Classical space and, moreover, can generate a diversity of visions instead of a unified view, must be considered. In order to consider this problem in a clear and efficient manner, I believe it is best to study not complex works of architecture, but the spaces of gardens which reveal their spatial outlines more simply and clearly.

In truth, I already had in my mind images of what I have repeatedly referred to up to now as Classical space and multi-layered space. In referring to Classical space, I have been imagining the space of French palatial gardens, and in the case of multi-layered space, I have been thinking of the space of Japanese tour gardens. That perhaps reveals the limits of human imagination and the difficulty of conjuring up what one has not already seen or experienced. Be that as it may, let us now investigate actual examples of those spaces in a detailed way.

Spatial differences between French and Japanese gardens
From the top floor of the château of Vaux-le-Vicomte located in a suburb of Paris, one can see magnificent French gardens organised around a vista beginning at the centre of the château and extending in a straight line over a large, nearly level property surrounded by woods. To the right and left of this vista or axis, defined by a central path, are many beautifully trimmed and evenly spaced borders, and between them are intersecting channels of water.

The beautiful gardens of Versailles are founded on balance and proportion; they are said to have been modelled on those of Vaux-le-Vicomte but were laid on an even larger area of land. There, the vista down the middle of the gardens is emphasised to an even greater degree. From the King's apartments in the centre of the palace one can see it stretching in a straight line, defined in its latter course by the Grand Canal which intersects with a cross-arm, and disappearing into the far distance where the sky meets land. One has the illusion that one's vision extends much further than is actually possible.

These French gardens are vast in area (those at Versailles are said to cover 300 hectares in all). The royalty and the nobility toured these gardens in carriages. Despite their large sizes, these gardens have extremely simple and clear organisations, making it easy to comprehend them in their entirety. In other words, in each case the spatial order is centred on one point, namely the centre of the château. If one stands at that point, then one can see all the gardens and, in that sense, integrate them. Since it is clear from any point in the gardens what the relationship of that point to the centre is, one can readily ascertain where one is and through an awareness of its relationship to the centre, understand the entire layout of the gardens from within the gardens as well.

The availability of an unobstructed view of the entire layout from any point within is what is most notably absent in the Japanese garden.

Shrubs, trees and rock arrangements overlap to obstruct the line of vision, creating shadows and eliminating vistas. One may work one's way past shrubs, circle a pond, cross a stone bridge arching over a stream, and walk over a stone-paved path, all in search of a vista, but the landscape changes in appearance from moment to moment as one moves; no vista appears.

The overlapping landscape bends one's line of vision and foils attempts to see the entire garden. The landscape is not integrated through vision but is in fact compelled to flex and fragment. This poverty of vista is precisely what is distinctive about a Japanese garden. The absence of *vista*, the *flexion* and *fragmentation* of vision instead of the integration of the whole by means of a sweeping view represents a positive, rather than a negative principle behind the Japanese garden.

Constructed and Deconstructed qualities of space

However, this principle has no direct relationship to the beauty or ugliness of a view, nor can one develop from it some general theory of Japanese, as opposed to European, culture. Nor do I have any intention of initiating a detailed study of gardens. My intention instead is to examine in a concrete way two sets of gardens, one with vistas and the other without, and by considering the meaning hidden behind human vision to investigate what spatial structure is implicit in that vision.

First, let us consider what a *vista*, which is absent in one type of garden and available at all points in the other, means. A French garden is not only extremely artificial but *constructed*. Its flowers and trees do not appeal to one's feelings about nature but rather constitute material subordinate to the entire plan. Form and material are clearly divorced, and the former completely dominates the latter. Consequently, materials are treated as unchanging and unrelated to the generative process. Although trees are continuously changing and being created, the consequences of such activity are not acknowledged; the trees are identified only as conical or cubic forms. All plants as plants have been banished from the garden, and it is only rectangles and circles that are arranged on the extensive, level site paved with gravel, creating a symmetrical, geometrical pattern. There is only a completely static surface that will remain forever unchanged.

To create a unified garden by compelling materials, whether they be trees or water, to take on unchanging forms with no concern for diversity or generative transformations represents the complete dominance of the intellect. The result is a highly *constructed* space.

Making the object insubstantial confers on it a *transparency* and endows vision with a privileged character. *Visual transparency* is a quality or state allowing one to penetrate all parts of the object. It is as if the source of light and power of vision residing within the self were situated God-like at the vertex of a cone-shaped world and the self could see into the furthest depths of the cone. No doubt, transparency according to the law of perspective approaches this conical situation.

We, as subjects that see, cannot, unlike God, separate ourselves completely from the diverse, actual world. This is because the self that gazes upon an object is itself a diverse, opaque presence full of distorting noise. The transparent cone that has been isolated from the infinitely pleated, diverse world is enveloped by the opacity of the self which gazes from the vortex and the opacity of that part of the world that the cone has ignored. One might almost say that transparency is a chance product born of these opaque pleats.

If the self continues to look through the cone, at some point everything undoubtedly will become transparent. Everything will become like glass, permitting light to pass through and making visible the back or the ground of a landscape. The world, however, will not have become truly transparent. It only means that the cone with the self at the vertex has been temporarily isolated. For the world to become truly transparent, the self that gazes must not be an opaque self but a point-like, insubstantial existence from which everything – substance and extension – has been eliminated. The act of looking and the world inside the cone must be decisively separated, because the homogeneity

of the expanse presenting itself to the eyes and the self is by no means always guaranteed. Control and cleaning must be undertaken to see that no noise or distortion enters the cone.

As soon as there is a disfigurement or distortion for some reason, it must be discovered and eliminated; each time new leaves appear on plants and grow unchecked, threatening to distort conical forms and other geometrical patterns, the gardener must wield his shears with utmost severity to correct even the slightest aberration. The planting in conical or cubic form constitutes an enclosure that confines meaning and prevents it from stirring, dissolving or straying. Consequently, a French garden where the spatial order converges on one point can be said to have only one landscape. The diversity or polysemy of landscape and vision is to be completely ignored. That is the basic principle behind a *constructed* garden.

But what happens when, unlike a French garden, the garden is uncropped and the landscape is left to sway and stir as it may? What would happen if, instead of heightening perception, enlarging the cone of vision, and thereby achieving integration of the landscape through transparency at a larger scale, vision travelled from one distorted fragment to another in accordance with shifts in the point of view or the actions of the body? A Japanese garden might be the result.

As has already been pointed out, the absence of vista is characteristic of a Japanese garden. This absence of vista is a consequence of the *multi-layered quality of the landscape*, evident in the planting, the rock arrangement and the trees, as at Tenryuji or Nanzenji. It is a well-known fact that even at the garden of Ryoanji, which seems so lucid at first glance, the rocks are arranged on the white sand so that not all 15 can be seen at once from the *en*, no matter what the angle. Rock obstructs rock and the landscape is always fragmented. Vision is not allowed to dominate the whole of this garden either. As in the garden of Tenryuji or Nanzenji, the landscape becomes a set of overlapping and contiguous landscapes that deviate slightly from each other. Multiple landscapes coexist.

As a result of overlapping, there are always parts that are hidden. A hidden part, if one changes one's viewpoint, becomes patent, and what had been visible now becomes latent. This mechanism makes it difficult to apprehend the entire garden. For the viewer, the landscape at each moment certainly exists in front of his eyes, but the plan of the whole is difficult to structure. It is difficult for him to measure his position relative to the entire garden or the distance to a given plant or rock, and without a clear order, multiple landscapes are generated as one's point of view shifts. The absence of a transcendent centre or vision that can give order to space robs a Japanese garden of perspective and transforms it into an *un-constructed* space.

However, the Japanese garden is after all an object deliberately created by man, and negative terms such as 'without order' or 'unconstructed' are surely inadequate descriptions. A Deconstructionist principle that actively promotes irregularity must be behind what appears at first glance to be without order. The *multi-layered, contiguous* landscapes constitute *parts*, but these parts do not simply and wilfully link themselves. Perhaps then there is something to be discovered in the way the parts are connected.

Dispersal and transparency in multi-layered space

It is first of all necessary to generate a transparency of vision through the movement of the point of view, from part to complementary part, from *fragment* to *fragment*, and from distortion to distortion. What is indispensable is not an order or a transparency within a conical field of vision but a transparency of vision that bundles together diverse and multiple objects as if into *mosaics, chains* and *meshes,* weaving these objects in different dimensions into a sort of patchwork.

In describing transparency in architectural space, Colin Rowe starts with the opacity of such a multi-layered condition and from it abstracts two types of transparency. He notes the following concept of transparency defined by Gyorgy Kepes:

  If one sees two or more figures overlapping one another, and each of them claims for itself the common overlapped part, then one is confronted with a contradiction of spatial dimensions. To resolve this contradiction one must assume the presence of a new optical quality. The figures are endowed with transparency: that is, they are able to interpenetrate without an optical destruction of each other. Transparency however implies more than an optical characteristic, it implies a broader spatial order. Transparency means a simultaneous perception of different spatial locations. Space not only recedes but fluctuates in a continuous activity. The position of the transparent figures has equivocal meaning as one sees each figure now as the closer, now as the further one.

From this Rowe posits the idea of transparency as a physical attribute (real or *literal transparency*) and transparency as a perceptual attribute or a particular characteristic of an organisation (*phenomenal transparency*). He further suggests that with regard to the physical attribute of materials, there is a transparency that differs from the total absence of opacity. According to this definition, transparency is not the opposite of opacity but signifies a more ambiguous condition.

Transparency in that sense is not a condition allowing visual penetration of a space with depth from a given point, but instead is a bundle of interpenetrating perceptions within a depthless space not conforming to the principle of perspective. For Rowe, it was Cubism that achieved a new transparency in paintings through dispersed perception:

A Cubist painting, with its overlapping layers of grids suggested by the horizontals and verticals of line segments and fragments, creates a space without depth. Gradually, the observer adds depth to this space and an image emerges. The depth of perspective is here replaced by geometrical, entangled grids without depth. Transparency is at last achieved, in a space that cannot be penetrated from one point, through a network of interpenetrating visions.

Transparency is achieved, not by means of a single, privileged position but by the interpenetration of diverse points, that is, solely through the transformation of vision. It is only through dispersal, distortion and transformation that structural transparency is attained. Vision pierces every corner of each discontinuous and distorted fragment and extends further the perceptual, structural mesh.

The generation of meaning by multi-layered space

The multi-layered garden is above all *metonymic*. This is because landscape is generated by *systematic activity* such as aberration, overlapping and transformation. One's gaze and the objects of vision are dispersed and slide in a zigzag path past fragments of a patchwork landscape where distances cannot be measured. The self is no longer certain of literal transparency. The landscape that had seemed transparent has everywhere become opaque; everywhere it flexes and bears drifting fragments. Here the landscape knows no confinement or cessation. Though one may try to apprehend the significance of each fragment or the whole, it forever eludes one.

Naturally it is impossible to discover and interpret the religious meaning of the landscape based on the teachings of history. From olden times it has been known that the pond symbolised the ocean and the rock arrangement in the pond an island or mountain in the ocean. In particular, the rock arrangement is the nucleus of the Japanese garden and symbolises the sacred mountain at the centre of the universe.

However, searching for a single meaning aided by signs that have turned into conventions is irrelevant to the issue I am presently addressing. The light moving over the distorted surface of the rocks, the overlapping fragments of landscape, the stir and commotion they give rise to, and the sound of flowing water – only half their meanings can be identified. The space of the generative garden is above all a place for generating meaning, and to reduce it to a religious or political interpretation would confine the generation of meaning.

Spatial or material expression does not represent a sort of transparent wrap thrown over whatever is meant. Our task is not interpretation but an examination of the way the opaque fabric that is polysemy is woven. Polysemy here does not mean simply that the space or garden has diverse aspects that can be interpreted in multiple ways but that the space or garden offers multiplicity itself, a multiplicity of irreducible meanings.

Do not diversity and polysemy themselves constitute the true character of language? Metonymy and metaphor are such attributes in amplified guise. Paul Ricoeur explains his motive for making metaphor the theme of his study, and states that trope is truly the creative and moreover lucid expression of language. He writes that this is notable precisely when language operates at the limits of its expressive capacity, and that it is also the function of trope to make possible the sorting of meaning so as to give life to a text.

Trope is not an ornament to everyday language but is instead language in its most vital, true guise before it has been weighed down with inertia. This characteristic found in trope is not limited to linguistic phenomena in a strict sense. It was of course Roman Jakobson who saw language as having two intersecting axes, that of associative relationships and that of relationships of *syntagme*, the former corresponding to metaphor and the latter to metonymy. This dualistic, contrasting relationship is not limited to language, according to Jakobson, who saw it in a wide range of human spiritual activities; the distinction between metaphorical expressions based on similarity and metonymic expressions based on contiguity is to be found in spatial arts such as paintings and motion pictures. Since Jakobson made his observations, metaphor and metonymy as polar opposite operations of language have become, not simply a textual issue of rhetoric, but a matter concerning the general process of expression.

Today, there is criticism of such a generalised bi-polar schema. For example, Ricoeur proposes, in place of a semiotic position that considers metaphor only on the basis of the laws of association-substitution, similarity and choice – an argument that would reconsider metaphor too as having a predicative character. If metaphor too should have a predicative character, then that would mean it constituted a *syntagme*. He asserts that the secret of metaphor is to be sought in relationships of *syntagme*, that is, in contextual connections.

Although the view that metaphor is based on similarity and metonymy on contiguity is still accepted, the two are seen not to function in an antinomic fashion; instead, at times they will form a latent association and at other times they will have a patent semantic effect based on *syntagme*.

To discover metaphoric or metonymic expressions in a space or a garden, on the basis of the above observations, is not in itself very difficult, for example, there are the already mentioned rock arrangement as sacred mountain and the pond as ocean or a sandy beach. However, a reading of the landscape aided solely by such similarities will result in conventionalised, banal stereotypes which is what all tropes are fated to become.

How does one distinguish between conventional metaphors, the intimated meanings of which are easily revealed, and metaphors that appear opaque and yield their meanings only by true discovery? As opposed to the former, which depends on the principles of similarity and substitution, the latter is introduced into a whole where metaphor and metonymy can coexist through latent polysemy or momentary semantic operations, as in the multi-layered spaces and gardens that have already been considered. Something like a predicative operation that generates fresh meaning so as to shape series and systems in the direction of *syntagme* is observable.

A word in itself has no meaning, much less multiple meanings. Meaning is generated only when the word is articulated with other words. Moreover, just as a word can take on different meanings depending on a situation, as Ricoeur pointed out, the multi-layered fragments of landscape have no inherent meanings, nor indeed are they even connected to established meanings. In a space or garden created after all out of matter, things cannot operate as smoothly as in language. However, multiple, fragmentary landscapes, wherein no vistas obtain, overlap, and the vision in each situation is connotatively shaped; in this space that approaches a multiplicity of contiguous and slightly divergent landscapes, metaphors are formed through similarity, substitution and choice. Metonymy is formed through a Cubist transparency that does not depend on penetration from a single, privileged point.

Naturally these two methods intermingle and generate the functions of *concatenation* and *system (syntagme)*. In such a space, we must chart one fragment after another, alternating between transparency and movement and traversing a multi-layered and diverse terrain.

Inscribing dispersed, multi-layered space

People who have thought of architecture as a form of expression and something that is designed will no doubt consider the notion of 'inscribing' architectural space strange. Here, 'inscribing' does not mean what it usually means; ie marking (as with words or characters) in order to express and to transmit some message or meaning. The transmission of a message or meaning is made possible by a conventionalised act or acts of expression (inscribing) that are based on a systematic code. However, inscribing as used here means creating an arrangement or a series of traces and differences that ought to be visible at the source when systems and codes have been stripped away or negated. Such a condition is a text of traces and differences and represents a mechanism for generating meaning. It is completely different from the mechanism for meanings that are transmitted through systematic codes.

I will discuss this matter in detail at another time and here will simply describe how I actually inscribed multi-layered, dispersed spaces. The diverse visions engendered by a multi-layered and dispersed quality of space represent an opaque transparency. In other words, they represent perceptions or visions generated by reversals and transfers within the depths of one's consciousness. A simple example of this is Rubin's diagrams in which the figure-ground relationships reverse themselves. However, the vision generated by a multi-layered, dispersed quality of space is not accounted for so simply. It is a vision generated by more complex conditions such as suppression, deficiency and compression that are related to the depths of the consciousness.

*   *   *

I will now discuss how I inscribed space on the basis of these ideas concerning vision. Space is taken to be a void that is a result of the reversal of a solid mass. To inscribe this, a grid of grooves is first cut into the solid mass of Fig 1(A), resulting in (B). This grooved grid is a sign that makes it possible to inscribe reversals and the displacement of 'deficiency'. It is also a trace for generating differences such as void and solid, and negative and positive.

The trace represented by the empty grooves can be considered the reverse, that is, the negative, of a solid, gridded frame (C). Thus, if space is inscribed using these signs – namely the grooves, which are negative, and the frame, which is positive – the result is Fig 1 (C). In other words, first the difference between positive and negative is inscribed into the solid of (A) using grooves. Next, the parts of (B) are reversed – so that negative grooves become a positive frame, and the positive solid becomes a negative void – resulting in the condition (C). The space generated by the reversal of a solid has been transformed by means of the grooves and the frame into a sign. That is what I mean by the inscribing of space.

Next, Fig 2 is an example of a space – which has been generated by the reversal of a solid – being inscribed by means of colour instead of grooves and a frame. Here white denotes what is void and black denotes what is solid. This merely follows the common practice of using white to represent what is 'absent' and black to represent what is 'present'. What is positive, that is, what is coloured black, can be taken to be the result of the reversal of what is negative, that is, what is coloured white. In the same way, white can be considered the result of the reversal of black. This leads to space being inscribed as in (C).

In Figs 3 and 4, a wall that is 'absent' and in reality not visible is inscribed using grooves and the colour white to represent what is negative. The walls shown in Fig 3 (A) and Fig 4 (A) are present; they are marked respectively by grooves and white stripes in order to create a difference between positive and negative. Next, the grooves are reversed and made solid, and what is white is reversed and made black, in order to reverse what is present in (A) to what is absent. Grooves become a solid frame, and solid becomes void. Where colour is used, similar reversals take place. In this way, absence is inscribed.

This method of inscribing an absent wall provides a way of inscribing any part of a wall that is made invisible by overlapping, as in Fig 5. In other words, a portion that cannot actually be seen because it is masked by another wall is inscribed – as in Fig 6, using a black, empty frame – as an absent wall generated by the reversal of presence. (It could also be inscribed by means of colours.) This is also a way of inscribing a transparency that is attributable to perception.

The method of inscription shown in Fig 6 is the basis for inscribing the layering of forms or spaces. For example, in Fig 7 a multi-layered space created by two present walls is inscribed. In Fig 8 a space created by layering a present wall and a wall that has already been inscribed as absent is inscribed. In Figs 9 and 10, spaces that are created by the layering of a wall that has been inscribed as absent with, respectively, a wall that is present and a wall that is absent are inscribed.

The above has been a discussion of the basic method of inscribing multi-layered space and examples of its application. Figs 11a and 11b are attempts to inscribe forms and spaces generated by what are perceived by the consciousness as deficiency and displacement. In Fig 11a a portion of a wall that is present is cut, and then this portion is depicted by dotted lines. In Fig 11b, the dotted portion is not really visible because it is deficient and displaced, but it is inscribed nevertheless as an absent wall because it is perceived by the consciousness as a wall that had once been there.

My projects Mizoe-1 and Mizoe-2 are based on the above method of inscription. Spaces are layered and walls cut and segmented. Both present and absent walls are divided and displaced repeatedly. Next the spaces in Mizoe-2 are generated by the process of layering and dispersal. The fragments generated by segmenting, layering, dividing and cutting walls are compounded to reach the final form.

ABOVE: MIZOE-1; *BELOW:* MIZOE-2

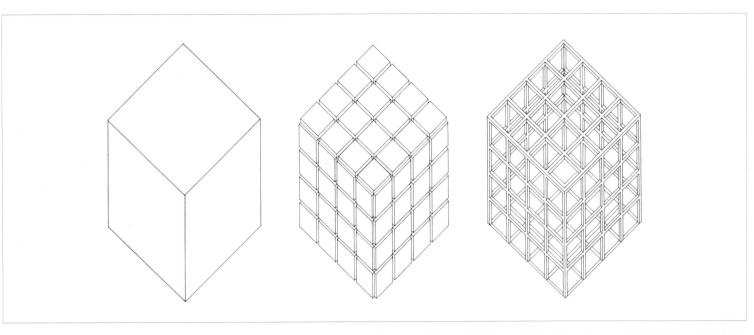

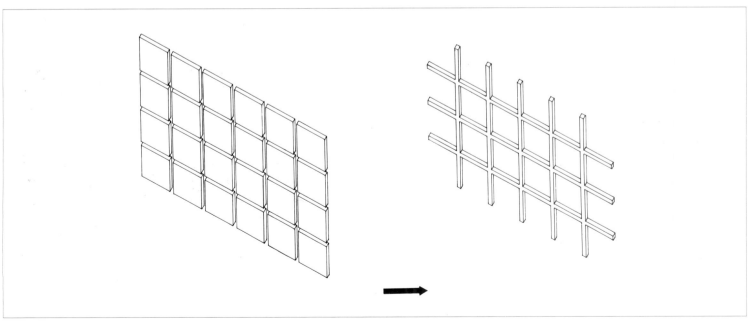

FROM TOP: FIG 1 a, b, c; FIG 2 a, b, c; FIG 3

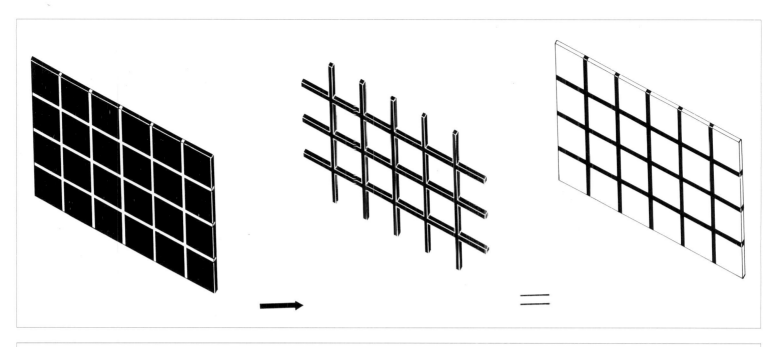

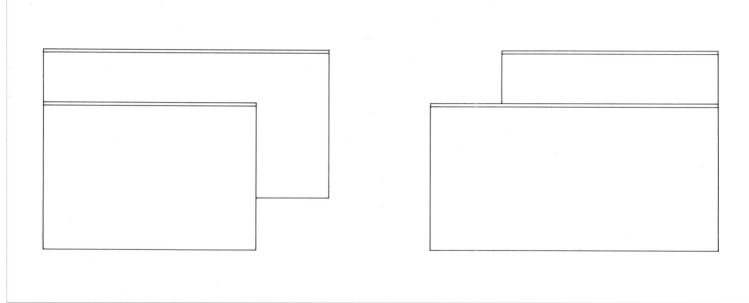

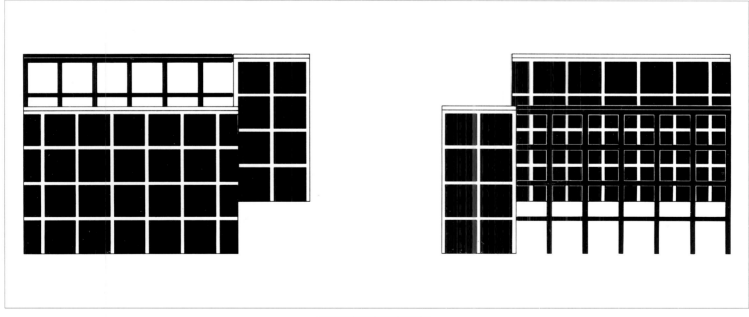

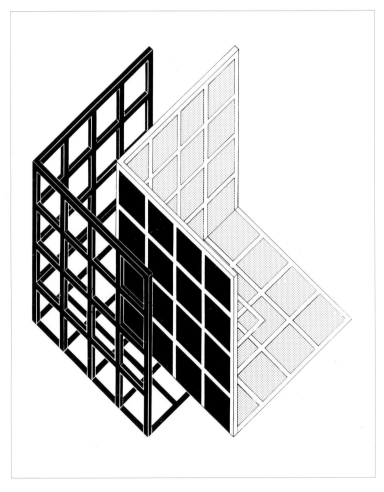

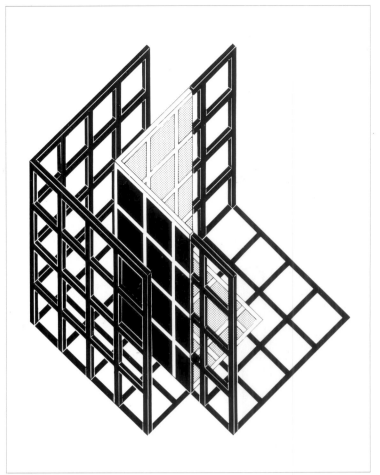

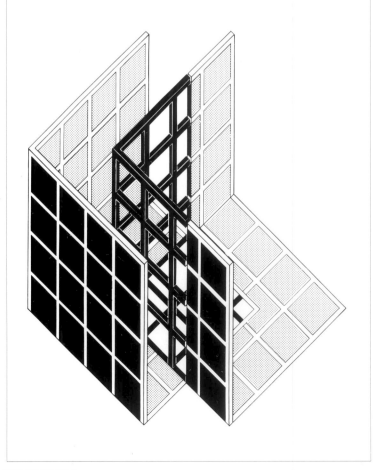

ABOVE L TO R: FIG 7; FIG 8; BELOW: FIG 9

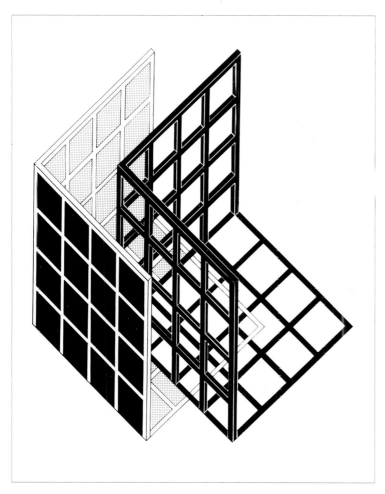

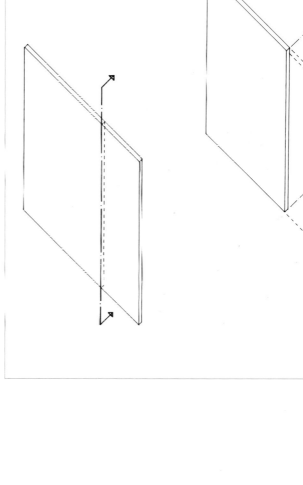

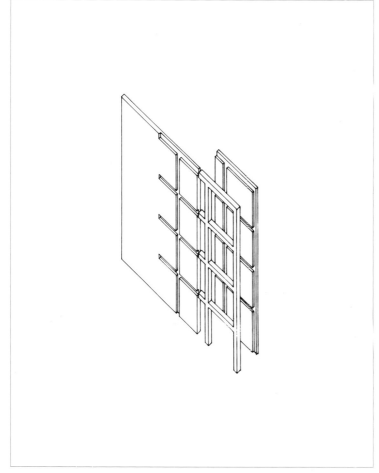

ABOVE L TO R: FIG 10; FIG 11a; BELOW: FIG 11b

STANLEY TIGERMAN, FUKUOKA CITY MIXED-USE APARTMENT BUILDING, KIUSHU, JAPAN, 1988-9, AXONOMETRIC

STANLEY TIGERMAN
Construction (De)Construction (Re) Construction
Architectural Antinomies and a (Re)newed Beginning

The (pre)*text* of American (Forget)*fulness*

The Amnesiac (pre)*Text* for an American Absence (exile) (under)*writes* ([under]*rights*) repeated attempts at healing an irreparable wound. Those continuously failed attempts result from an initial failure to heal the original contamination seeded at the site of Eden. The insistance to heal the unhealable results in perpetual attempts to deflect life's trajectory away from its inevitable, (ir)*reducible* end.

MEMBER **1	(DIS)MEMBER**2	(RE)MEMBER**3
CONSTRUCTION	(de)CONSTRUCTION	(re)CONSTRUCTION
ZIMZUM	SHEVIRATH HAKELIM	TIKKUN

*If the six-pointed star is an ancient symbol for healing, why does 'time heal all wounds'?

**Members* of the human race are (dis)*member*ed through their participation in, observation – or tacit acknowledgement of – a holocaust, which they all (sub)/(un)*consciously* (re)*member*. At Masada, in memory of its downfall, and in memory of all subsequent downfalls, newly initiated *members* of the Israeli army (re)*member* (dis)*member*ment by swearing the oath 'never again'.

The (sub)text of Kabbalistic interpretation (a)

(a) From Harold Bloom's interpretation of Lurianic Kabbalistic typology: *A Map of Misreading*, p5, (parentheses are my own).

ZIMZUM*	SHEVIRATH HAKELIM**	TIKKUN***

* ZIMZUM is the Creator's withdrawal or contraction so as to make possible a creation (*member*) that is not (him)*self*.

** SHEVIRATH HAKELIM is the breaking-apart-of-the-vessels ([dis]*member*), a vision of creation-as-catastrophe

***TIKKUN is restitution or restoration ([re]*member*) – man's contribution to God's work.

1 Member n. 1 A person belonging to an incorporated or organised body, society, etc: a member of Congress, a member of a club. 2 A limb or other functional organ of an animal body. 3 A part or element of a structural or composite whole, distinguishable from other parts or elements, as a part of a sentence, syllogism, period, or discourse, or any necessary part of a structural framework, as a tie rod, post or strut in the truss of a bridge. 4 A subordinate classificatory part: A species is a member of a genus. 5 Bot. A part of a plant considered with reference to position and structure, but regardless of function. 6 Math. a Either side of an equation. b A set of figures or symbols forming part of a formula or number. c Any one of the items forming a series.

2 Dis-member v. 1 To cut or pull limb or part from part. 2 To divide; separate into parts and distribute, as an empire.

3 Re-member v. 1 To bring back or present again to the mind or memory: recall; recollect. 2 To keep in mind carefully, as for a purpose. 3 To bear in mind with affection, respect, awe, etc. 4 To bear in mind as worthy of a reward, gift, etc: She remembered me in her will. 5 To reward: tip: Remember the steward. 6 Obs. To remind. 7 To have or use one's memory.

Modernism	(post)Modernism	(re)Postmodernism
		(Riposte)
Construction	(de)Construction	(re)Construction
Production 1	Destruction	(re)Production 2
Present 3	Absent	(re)Present 4

1 Production n. 1 The act of process or producing. 2 In political economy, a producing for use, involving the creating or increasing of economic wealth: in contradistinction to consumption (by use). 3 That which is produced or made; any tangible result of industrial, artistic or literary labour.

2 Re-production n. 1 The act or power of reproducing. 2 Biol. The process by which an animal or plant gives rise to another of its kind; generation. 3 Psychol. *The process of the memory by which objects that have previously been known are brought back into consciousness* (italics are my own). 4 That which is reproduced, as a revival in drama or a copy in art.

3 present adj. 1 Being in a place or company referred to or contemplated; being at hand; opposed to absent. 2 Now going on; current; not past or future. 3 Actually in mind. 4 Immediately impending or actually going on; not delayed; instant. 5 Relating to or signifying what is going on at the time being; the present tense, present participle. 6 Ready at hand; prompt in emergency; a present wit, a present aid. **n** 1 Present time; now; the time being. 2 gram. The present tense; also, a verbal form denoting it. 3 A present matter or affair; a question under consideration. 4 pl. law Present writings: term for the document in which the word occurs: Know all men by these presents.

4 Re-present vt. To serve as the symbol, expression or designation of; symbolise: The letters of the alphabet represent the sounds of speech. 2 To express or symbolise in this manner: to represent royal power with a sceptre. 3 To set forth a likeness or image of; depict; portray, as in painting or sculpture. 4 a To produce on the stage, as an opera. b To act the part of; impersonate, as a character in a play. 5 To serve as or be the delegate, agent, etc, of: He represents the State of Maine. 6 To describe as being of a specified character or condition: They represented him as a genius. 7 To set forth in words; state; explain: He represented the circumstances of his case. 8 To bring before the mind; present clearly. 9 To serve as an example, specimen, type, etc, of; typify: His use of words represents an outmoded school of writing.

Structuralism   (post)*Structuralism*   (re)*Poststructuralism*
                                                       Riposte *Structuralism*
                                                       (re)*Claim**
                                                       (re)*Cover**
                                                       (re)*New**
                                                       (re)*Store**

The (con)text of the initial wound (original sin)

*Acknowledging the presence of a wound (and expressing that admission by perpetually [re]*presenting* that wound [cut, *couper*] by the scar that signifies it), does not relieve one from the recurring responsibility that defines human behaviour, such that it continuously attempts to heal it. Even so, it is literally impossible to overcome the knowledge that the wound can never, finally, be healed without resorting to plastic surgery, which is here interpreted to mean the suppression of the memory of the wound (self-inflicted amnesia) – ie, faith – assuring its (dis)*appearance*. The original wound – the fall from a state of grace in paradise – requires recognition – not suppression. Faith renders any further interpretation of the original wound unnecessary, therefore serving to mute memory. Finally, the same precise faith nullifies any sense of responsibility to (re)*write* – indeed to (re)*right* – that original failure, without (re)*moving* that failure from memory.

Rather than merely acting out iterations of mimesis through repetition, Americans attempt to (re)*produce* originary evidence, so as to 'get it right' the next time; even though they know (sub)*consciously* that 'it' can neither be 'righted', nor that one can ever 'get it right'. By yearning for an intersection with lost origins – for an absent beginning – Americans try (even though they repeatedly fail) to (re)*gain* lost time (never thinking that they may be out of time).

Even though belief in a present tempered by a future perceived as an opportunity to make things better, ie, to gain lost time, (re)*presentation* infers a better time. By superimposing the concept of time on to the present, (re)*presentation* is rationalised. While it is well within the ethics of architecture's domain to attempt to accomplish this, the recognition that failure is perpetually imminent has only marginal acceptability within conventional architectural traditions. The very same traditions that mute the memory of original sin. After all, architecture has long been at the service of perpetual value systems . . . otherwise, Plato could never have accused it (art) as being in the shadow of truth.

(re)*Production* verifies one's belief in the original product. (re)*Production* is an implicit admission that the original product has value through legitimation by attempting to make that original product better by repeatedly (re)*making* it (the purpose of cross-fertilisation, indeed the purpose underlying the conceiving of a child implies that the next iteration will be better than the originating one). (re)*Production* also exploits the passage of time to heal the wound of the entrance into the world of a (re)*produced* product. Evidence to the contrary notwithstanding, the concept of attempting to improve a situation contradicts the cynical view that (no)*thing* ever gets better – it is only different. This is where cross-fertilisation intersects with architecture. Each is seminally informed by the opinion intrinsic to both . . . I take this optimism to signify acts of attempts at healing.

'While Hegel maintains that when love is truly conceived, "the wounds of spirit heal and leave no scars", Heidegger insists that the rending of difference can never be totally healed.'

(*Altarity* 51)

Belief*   (dis)*Belief***   (re)*lief****
                                       (Re)*new*ed Belief

* With Hegel, a long ontotheological tradition comes to an end, through 'synthesis' (or is it [sin]*Thesis*?) – a mechanism that generally suborns 'thesis', but more particularly suppresses '(anti)*thesis*', in favour of (re)*solving* (and presumably amalgamating), both. The 'scab' of antithesis is permitted to heal (the scar of synthesis only

retains reluctantly the palimpsest of the scab of antithesis). Plastic surgery in the guise of faith manifested in synthesis removes the trace of the wound of antithesis, whose continued presence would otherwise be (un)*bearable* in its (un)*resolved* perpetuation, indeed in its insistent (re)*interpretation*. For Hegel, no further interpretation of the sacred text is required – faith, or belief – first (dis)*places*, then (re)*places* exegesis, since the contravention of antithesis is removed. Textuality ceases to be an irritation – antithesis, and with it interpretation, is (dis)*placed* into a hiatic state of limbo only awaiting (re)*activation*.

** Americans inherit a post-Nietszchean world where first the sacred other – God – then the sacred self – man – is murdered. Belief first in a divine being, and then by extension, in any being, is (dis)*placed* by (dis)*belief*. Self is (re)*placed* by an equal 'otherness' in an (un)*solvable* equation (un)*burdened* by ethical considerations. Originally, the sacred other and the sacred self were on opposite sides of a primary equation, where, by each requiring the other, a false state of parity was artificially induced. The introduction of (dis)*belief* (dis)*locates* the original equation, and with that (dis)*locative* introduction, (dis)*places* parity, just as it (dis)*places* first God, and then, as it irrevocably displaces man in a place that is (no)*place*.

*** Born of other strains, the attempt to produce one better than the original through cross-fertilisation is called 'hybrid' or 'child'.

Belief	(dis)*Belief*	(re)*lief*
		(re)*New*ed Belief
Vest	(di)Vest	(re)Vest
Tract	(dis)Tract	(re)Tract
Tort	(dis)Tort	(re)Tort
Solve	(de)Solve	(re)Solve
Sign	(de)Sign	(re)Sign
Assemble	(dis)Semble	(re)Semble
Prove	(dis)Prove	(re)Prove
Plenish	(de)Plenish	(re)Plenish
Orient	(dis)Orient	(re)Orient
Generate	(de)Generate	(re)Generate
Inform	(de)Form	(re)Form
Fit	(mis)Fit	(re)Fit
Direct	(mis)Direct	(re)Direct
Claim	(dis)Claim	(re)Claim
Compose	(de)Compose	(re)Compose
Cast	(mis)Cast	(re)Cast
Reading	(mis)Reading	(re)Reading
Appropriate	(mis)Appropriate	(re)Appropriate
Count	(dis)Count	(re)Count
Course	(dis)Course	(re)Course
Centring	(de)Centring	(re)Centring
Nomination	(de)Nomination	(re)Nomination
Location	(dis)Location	(re)Location
Placement	(dis)Placement	(re)Placement
Construction	(de)*Construction*	(re)*Construction*
Cover	(dis)Cover	(re)Cover
Evaluation	(de)Valuation	(re)Valuation
Activate	(de)Activate	(re)Activate
Formation	(de)Formation	(re)Formation

*Home**	*Exile***	*Home Away From Home****

* Heideggerian version of '*Bauen*', '*Bilded*', '*Bilden*'.

** See *The Architecture of Exile* by S Tigerman, Rizzoli, New York, 1988.

*** Replacement of a displaced place.

The (re)*Pressed* Text of American Architecture

Increasingly, as the 20th century nears completion, it is becoming painfully clear that the (im)*possible* search for an intrinsic American architecture has been (dis)*located* in a time marked by time (marking time), and at a place signifying (no)*place*, of (im)*probable* closure. That clarity reveals a (dis)*junction* symbolic of the site of an American absence (re)*presenting* the inheritance of an emptiness learned originally just outside the east gate of Eden. The primary element that always expresses the constituent features of any epoch – language – is currently (de)*limited* in despair by utterances (dis)*located* from both theocentric, as well as anthropocentric, values.

Linguistic codes exert power through expression (the same codes however, also exert power through suppression). They influence (im)*measurably* beyond the elements that they nominally define. (de)*Coded*, like Samson shorn, they appear to simply state facts even as they inadvertently reveal the magic of the moment.

In America, a land composed virtually entirely of successive generations of exiles, the yearning to return to an original innocent state as a failed (re)*placement* of inhabiting successfully an alien and resisting 'rooting' instincts, now has a corresponding set of linguistic codes that are utilised in order to express the (dis)*junctive* nature of our time. Denials now (dis)*place* originary definitions that, in the beginning, rooted mankind to being through dwelling to existence in a home always at home. The cynicism of sophistication (age) has (re)*placed* the spontaneity of innocence (youth). But it wasn't always that way in a more childlike America, new and before its free/fall from grace.

The (co)*incidence* between the guileless optimism of a young nation, and a discipline such as architecture (whose tradition resonates with characteristic optimism) is tacitly understood. That (co)*incidence* is powered by the courage to accept a belief system perpetually (re)*activated* by 'newness'.

Modernism may have actually begun in the Renaissance as a condition of appropriation, but it was never enjoyed (nor exploited) more than by a nation of innocent exiles who, if they were to be true to their instinctive optimism, had no choice but to (re)*direct* their unsought condition constructively in 'modern ways'. The very word – *Modernism* – implies a condition of amnesia about the past, a determined attachment to the present, even while tilting slightly toward the future. Dialectically, however, Modernism also implies a challenge to a (pre)*Modern* condition inadvertently clarifying Modernism while appearing to stand over and against it. Modernism, after all, found a welcoming home in a childlike, youthful America free from cunning, (un)*informed* by deceit, (un)*tainted* by sophistication, an America for whom the present meant everything, and where (forget)*fulness* about history seemed essential to young Americans schizophrenically revelling in their (pre)*mimetic* innocence, even as they desperately desired parity with others who, they hoped, perceived them as the newest sophisticates.

The (text)*ure* of antinomy
A synthesis ([sin]*Thesis*) of continuously (un)*resolved* (op)*positions* based on the (ir)*reconcilability* of seemingly necessary inferences or conclusions (antinomy) seems (un)*likely* in an age dually devoted to either self-verification through the uses of the past, or to an (un)*conditional* indulgence in the (un)*predictability* of the future. Both strategies (dis)*locate* equally a belief in the power of the present. The resulting ambivalence elevates (dis)*junction* to a positional primacy of domination, and seems to suggest that the intrinsic quality of presence has an (un)*resolvably* slippery Janus-face that locks either backward or forward, but is so waferlike that it cannot speak meaningfully of its own time. The sound emanating from the face of the present is either Babel-like, or mute, giving way alternatively to the cacophony of the past and/or to the vast silences of the future. Simultaneously, by speaking (dis)*cordantly* of other times and other places, the voice of contemporaneity is strangled. We seem (un)*able* to articulate a present paradoxically (de)*void* of the inspiration to 'blow its own horn'.

We should know that looking backwards for verification only results in the wrenching frustration of an exile haplessly yearning for an (ir)*retrievable* original innocence, attainable only in memory, through (un)*fulfilled* desire. (Op)*positionally*, we should understand that, by 'throwing the baby out with the bathwater', a future without its past is only fictively compelling (and even that is temporary), since we are also reminded that 'we (can)*not* not know history'. Both polar positions are (un)*promising*, since neither is possible (with)*out* knowledge of the other. Each is contaminated by its (op)*posite*, thus neither is particularly innocent. Bookended by positions describing a condition of antinomy, the present is drained of itself shifting its weight so that it lies tantilisingly always just out of reach. 'Movement' or 'mobility' (the oscillation between [op]*positions*), becomes the dominant currency of an otherwise vacuous, state of contemporaneity.

Perhaps contemporary America is not a generative source of indigenous architecture after all. An American absentation may be ascribed to the fact that this country is neither old enough to legitimate, nor young enough to retrieve, visions otherwise located elsewhere. On the one hand, America's absence may be inextricably tied to the power of its pluralistic precedents which, for many, are rooted to a place that is multitudinously 'other' than any single one that could, in other circumstances, be called 'home'. The power of originary evidence, to which many Americans still yearn (and with it, the (re)*iterative* power of mimesis), overwhelms sensing possibilities tied to an (other)*wise* (dis)*illusioning* present. On the other hand, by thrusting one's self into the (un)*known* without the (re)*assurance* of precedent (to say nothing of the comfort of convention), the (dis)*junctiveness* of that thinness of time which is uniquely and solely ours is (re)*enforced*, perpetuating an *absent present*.

The continuous search for a point of origination in order to project form metaphorised by the Edenic tree of life is, in America, a 'Faery Land' without roots, perhaps even without a native soil which would otherwise nourish thoughts of 'home', or 'dwelling', or 'being'. It is precisely in response to being an American in an age where absence is characterised by removal from 'playing the game', that causes one's gaze to stray to places and pleasures behind, or in front of, one's position in time and in place. The suspension of belief in an American presence dislocates value as well as illusion in the power, indeed the existence, of a perpetual American dream. That particular (dis)*junction* (re)*locates* the power of the performer of presence to the selections of the spectator of absence, resulting in the domination of the voyeur over the player.

Thus the energy (or is it enervation?) of continuous contemporary (dis)*location* is bookended by a never-to-be-retrieved past, and a never-to-be-fulfilled future. The inference that a (dis)*junctive* present is inevitable is seeded by the (im)*possibility* of fulfilment by moving either forward or backward, and (re)*enforces* a gripping pause that is marked by (de)*constructive* marginalia. The death of God combines with the death of man (fore)*closing* whatever optimism that might be otherwise intrinsic to a *present* that has *presence*. The absence of either 'ethical norms or moral forms' conveys a chimeric freedom that exploits the loss of the power of presence. That imaginary (dis)*closure* presents instead a perpetually contaminated closure signifying the illusion that (im)*perfection* is its own reward – the paradox of the absent present – (de)*construction*.

By elevating interpretation to an (un)*precedented* level of (dis)*belief* (or freedom, depending on your view), not only is faith exacerbated, but ethics are excised in a country desperately in need of values in order to mark its maturity. The absence of ethical values (super)*imposed* on a state of incessant interpretation, projects a false sense of (in)*dependence* (in)*consistent* with the development of an individual, or collective, sense of self.

* * *

If Hegel's (pro)*position* of the trinity of first Greek, (dis)*placed* by Jew, and (re)*placed* by Christian is modified so that the original.

(un)*tampered* belief in god(s) is (dis)*placed* by man's challenge to his monotheistic God through the elevation of the self in order to engage in dialogue with God (the wound of continuous interpretation), and when that finally fails and man is expelled from paradise, man's efforts to make restitution in order to make the world better by attempting to heal an (un)*healable* rift, then a new (pro)*position* (re)*placing* 'faith' (plastic surgery) comes to pass. The palimpsest of the original wound is revealed – an erasure's trace – made present by the presence of a scar which (re)*presents* the signature, or name, by which the *attempt* at healing becomes evident. Time is crucial to the understanding of healing, for without the passing of time, mankind's (in)*ability* to sustain pain would not exist resulting in an (un)*endurable*, continuous, pain. The passage of time (combined with man's amnesia about it) allows for a scab to metamorphose into a scar. Since the mind cannot sustain pain, a scar is a mark that can be interpreted as signifying original pain, while at the same time the scar (re)*presents* the erasure of that original pain.

The original wound can never be healed by excision, or removal, but an attempt at (re)*conciliation* is necessary to (re)*present* faith in being, existing, dwelling. The scar remains so that one may not ever forget that there was a wound in the first place. A scar bears the trace of a scab, troubled by time. A scab (re)*presents* the initial sign of the process of healing. When a scab is ripped off, the wound that it marked is (re)*opened*, new blood is shed, and the original pain is (re)*membered*. The scar cannot be (re)*opened* without the creation of a new wound (super)*imposed* by new pain. But its perpetual presence (re)*members* the member that was originally ruptured through a process nominally called (dis)*memberment*. Time is crucial to a sequence of healing that begins by rupturing a (pre)*existing* condition, and ends with the memory of the enactment of a failed attempt to (re)*enliven* that lost, originary pain.

The (Sub)Text (Super)Imposed On The (Con)Text

The corrolation between the Lurianically interpreted Kabbalistical tryptich (*Zimzum, Shevirath Hakelim, Tikkun*) and their apparently coincidental architectural counterparts (*construction*, (de)*construction*, (re)*construction*) can no longer be ignored.

The history of Western architecture is indelibly stained by an obstinate optimism traced solely by constructive attitudes signified by construction. (in)*Formed* by anthropocentrism, architects have obligated themselves mimetically to repeat the paradisic (un)*equal* hierarchical relationship by subordinating self to that first perfect architect – God – by whose hand man's initial, and only ideal, home – the Garden of Eden – was conceived. Traditionally, the overwhelming desire to 'get it right' has been (re)*presented* by buildings suppressing any trace of a 'wound' (or, for that matter, (re)*pressing* the passage of time – and with it – suppressing the only hope of healing that wound). The sign of intrinsic optimism was manifest in construction, ie, that belief in being, or existence, that the Bible (later [re]*written* by

Heidegger) addresses.

Whatever the nature of construction – its style, its context, its bias – the implicit optimism of the human spirit innocently, if (in)*advertently*, suppressed 'mistakes' so as to mimetically express mankind's (un)*equal*, and (im)*perfect*, relationship to a divine being. Equal to Luria's Kabbalistical interpretation of 'Zimzum' (God's withdrawal, making way for mankind), anthropocentrism, ie, the inference of mankind's assuming 'centre stage', to better act out this primary (in)*equality*, was effected. Edenically, Zimzum can be interpreted as God's establishing of authority by the Genesis divine denial ('do not eat of the tree in the centre of the garden') which (through God's withdrawal), leaves 'centre stage' available for Adam and Eve to either obey, or to overturn, that mandate. Either way, Adam and Eve are given a primary message by God (un)*alterably* demanding a response. God's withdrawal makes Adam's and Eve's presence possible. By responding at all (never mind which response), Adam and Eve establish their own presence, which in turn, signifies God's absence – or – His withdrawal.

Similarly, the establishing of a corresponding architecture – one that responds mimetically to that first, perfect place made by the hand of God (Eden) – not only commits architecture to a perpetually (im)*perfect* condition, but ironically (re)*moves* the trace of that (im)*perfection* as it suppresses any possibility of erring in favour of 'getting it right'. The very nature of architecture since that time is couched in the (pre)*tension* of the architect trying to get it right by reducing the passage of time to a condition of absence – conscious removal.

As an architectural analogue to Zimzum and as an epilogue to the passion play of Christianity, the architect assumes a position of presence – a kind of divine (re)*placement* - so as to 'create' mimetically derived iterations of an imagined innocent state equated with perfection. For almost 2,000 years architects have denied the 'trace' of that perpetual wound which nostalgically draws mankind back to an originally innocent state. (im)*Possible* to attain, (il)*logical* to conceive, architects nonetheless persistently strive to reduce the distance between the problems of mimesis as they attempt to concretise divine ideals into a never-to-be-achieved state of innocence.

God's withdrawal allows mankind to (dis)*place* Him, and by their own (re)*placement*, they attempt to accomplish similar goals. With the coming of Christianity, faith or belief in an ideal (re)*enforces* architects' resolve as they attempt to (re)*place* a heavenly garden inhabited by 'named' creatures with a mimetically conceived divine city resurrecting mankind from the original fall from grace. While Christian faith is the final, synthesising element in Hegel's tripartite philosophical project (first Greek, then Jew and, finally, Christian), it becomes the first in a new tripartite series (Zimzum), followed by the apocolyptical view of the world metaphorised by the breaking of the vessels (Shevirath Hakelim), and concluded by continuously failed attempts to heal an irreparable wound (Tikkun).

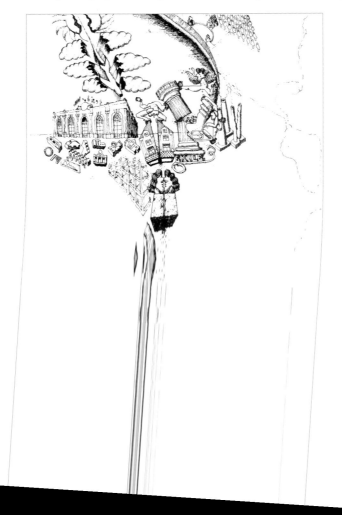

painfully clear that the (im)*possible* search for an intrinsic American architecture has been (dis)*located* in a time marked by time (marking time), and at a place signifying (no)*place*, of (im)*probable* closure. That clarity reveals a (dis)*junction* symbolic of the site of an American absence (re)*presenting* the inheritance of an emptiness learned originally just outside the east gate of Eden. The primary element that always expresses the constituent features of any epoch – language – is currently (de)*limited* in despair by utterances (dis)*located* from both theocentric, as well as anthropocentric, values.

Linguistic codes exert power through expression (the same codes however, also exert power through suppression). They influence (im)*measurably* beyond the elements that they nominally define. (de)*Coded*, like Samson shorn, they appear to simply state facts even as they inadvertently reveal the magic of the moment.

In America, a land composed virtually entirely of successive generations of exiles, the yearning to return to an original innocent state as a failed (re)*placement* of inhabiting successfully an alien and resisting 'rooting' instincts, now has a corresponding set of linguistic codes that are utilised in order to express the (dis)*junctive* nature of our time. Denials now (dis)*place* originary definitions that, in the beginning, rooted mankind to being through dwelling to existence in a home always at home. The cynicism of sophistication (age) has (re)*placed* the spontaneity of innocence (youth). But it wasn't always that way in a more childlike America, new and before its free/fall from grace.

The (co)*incidence* between the guileless optimism of a young nation, and a discipline such as architecture (whose tradition resonates with characteristic optimism) is tacitly understood. That (co)*incidence* is powered by the courage to accept a belief system perpetually (re)*activated* by 'newness'.

Modernism may have actually begun in the Renaissance as a condition of appropriation, but it was never enjoyed (nor exploited) more than by a nation of innocent exiles who, if they were to be true to their instinctive optimism, had no choice but to (re)*direct* their unsought condition constructively in 'modern ways'. The very word – *Modernism* – implies a condition of amnesia about the past, a determined attachment to the present, even while tilting slightly toward the future. Dialectically, however, Modernism also implies a challenge to a (pre)*Modern* condition inadvertently clarifying Modernism while appearing to stand over and against it. Modernism, after all, found a welcoming home in a childlike, youthful America free from cunning, (un)*informed* by deceit, (un)*tainted* by sophistication, an America for whom the present meant everything, and where (forget)*fulness* about history seemed essential to young Americans schizophrenically revelling in their (pre)*mimetic* innocence. even as they desperately desired parity with others who, they hoped, perceived them as the newest sophisticates.

The (text)*ure* of antinomy

A synthesis ([sin]*Thesis*) of continuously (un)*resolved* (op)*positions* based on the (ir)*reconcilability* of seemingly necessary inferences or conclusions (antinomy) seems (un)*likely* in an age dually devoted to either self-verification through the uses of the past, or to an (un)*conditional* indulgence in the (un)*predictability* of the future. Both strategies (dis)*locate* equally a belief in the power of the present. The resulting ambivalance elevates (dis)*junction* to a positional primacy of domination, and seems to suggest that the intrinsic quality of presence has an (un)*resolvably* slippery Janus-face that looks either backward or forward, but is so waferlike that it cannot speak meaningfully of its own time. The sound emanating from the face of the present is either Babel-like, or mute, giving way alternatively to the cacophony of the past and/or to the vast silences of the future. Simultaneously, by speaking (dis)*cordantly* of other times and other places, the voice of contemporaneity is strangled. We seem (un)*able* to articulate a present paradoxically (de)*void* of the inspiration to 'blow its own horn'.

We should know that looking backwards for verification only results in the wrenching frustration of an exile haplessly yearning for an (ir)*retrievable* original innocence, attainable only in memory, through (un)*fulfilled* desire. (Op)*positionally*, we should understand that, by 'throwing the baby out with the bathwater', a future without its past is only fictively compelling (and even that is temporary), since we are also reminded that 'we (can)*not* not know history'. Both polar positions are (un)*promising*, since neither is possible (with)*out* knowledge of the other. Each is contaminated by its (op)*posite*, thus neither is particularly innocent. Bookended by positions describing a condition of antinomy, the present is drained of itself shifting its weight so that it lies tantilisingly always just out of reach. 'Movement' or 'mobility' (the oscillation between [op]*positions*), becomes the dominant currency of an otherwise vacuous, state of contemporaneity.

Perhaps contemporary America is not a generative source of indigenous architecture after all. An American absentation may be ascribed to the fact that this country is neither old enough to legitimate, nor young enough to retrieve, visions otherwise located elsewhere. On the one hand, America's absence may be inextricably tied to the power of its pluralistic precedents which, for many, are rooted to a place that is multitudinously 'other' than any single one that could, in other circumstances, be called 'home'. The power of originary evidence, to which many Americans still yearn (and with it, the (re)*iterative* power of mimesis), overwhelms sensing possibilities tied to an (other)*wise* (dis)*illusioning* present. On the other hand, by thrusting one's self into the (un)*known* without the (re)*assurance* of precedent (to say nothing of the comfort of convention), the (dis)*junctiveness* of that thinness of time which is uniquely and solely ours is (re)*enforced*, perpetuating an *absent present*.

The continuous search for a point of origination in order to project form metaphorised by the Edenic tree of life is, in America, a 'Faery Land' without roots, perhaps even without a native soil which would otherwise nourish thoughts of 'home', or 'dwelling', or 'being'. It is precisely in response to being an American in an age where absence is characterised by removal from 'playing the game', that causes one's gaze to stray to places and pleasures behind, or in front of, one's position in time and in place. The suspension of belief in an American presence dislocates value as well as illusion in the power, indeed the existence. of a perpetual American dream. That particular (dis)*junction* (re)*locates* the power of the performer of presence to the selections of the spectator of absence, resulting in the domination of the voyeur over the player.

Thus the energy (or is it enervation?) of continuous contemporary (dis)*location* is bookended by a never-to-be-retrieved past, and a never-to-be-fulfilled future. The inference that a (dis)*junctive* present is inevitable is seeded by the (im)*possibility* of fulfilment by moving either forward or backward, and (re)*enforces* a gripping pause that is marked by (de)*constructive* marginalia. The death of God combines with the death of man (fore)*closing* whatever optimism that might be otherwise intrinsic to a *present* that has *presence*. The absence of either 'ethical norms or moral forms' conveys a chimeric freedom that exploits the loss of the power of presence. That imaginary (dis)*closure* presents instead a perpetually contaminated closure signifying the illusion that (im)*perfection* is its own reward – the paradox of the absent present – (de)*construction*.

By elevating interpretation to an (un)*precedented* level of (dis)*belief* (or freedom, depending on your view), not only is faith exacerbated, but ethics are excised in a country desperately in need of values in order to mark its maturity. The absence of ethical values (super)*imposed* on a state of incessant interpretation, projects a false sense of (in)*dependence* (in)*consistent* with the development of an individual, or collective. sense of self.

*   *   *

If Hegel's (pro)*position* of the trinity of first Greek, (dis)*placed* by Jew, and (re)*placed* by Christian is modified so that the original, (un)*tampered* belief in god(s) is (dis)*placed* by man's challenge to his monotheistic God through the elevation of the self in order to engage in dialogue with God (the wound of continuous interpretation), and when that finally fails and man is expelled from paradise, man's efforts to make restitution in order to make the world better by attempting to heal an (un)*healable* rift, then a new (pro)*position* (re)*placing* 'faith' (plastic surgery) comes to pass. The palimpsest of the original wound is revealed – an erasure's trace – made present by the presence of a scar which (re)*presents* the signature, or name, by which the *attempt* at healing becomes evident. Time is crucial to the understanding of healing, for without the passing of time, mankind's (in)*ability* to sustain pain would not exist resulting in an (un)*endurable*, continuous, pain. The passage of time (combined with man's amnesia about it) allows for a scab to metamorphose into a scar. Since the mind cannot sustain pain, a scar is a mark that can be interpreted as signifying original pain, while at the same time the scar (re)*presents* the erasure of that original pain.

The original wound can never be healed by excision, or removal, but an attempt at (re)*conciliation* is necessary to (re)*present* faith in being, existing, dwelling. The scar remains so that one may not ever forget that there was a wound in the first place. A scar bears the trace of a scab, troubled by time. A scab (re)*presents* the initial sign of the process of healing. When a scab is ripped off, the wound that it marked is (re)*opened*, new blood is shed, and the original pain is (re)*membered*. The scar cannot be (re)*opened* without the creation of a new wound (super)*imposed* by new pain. But its perpetual presence (re)*members* the member that was originally ruptured through a process nominally called (dis)*memberment*. Time is crucial to a sequence of healing that begins by rupturing a (pre)*existing* condition, and ends with the memory of the enactment of a failed attempt to (re)*enliven* that lost, originary pain.

The (Sub)Text (Super)Imposed On The (Con)Text

The corrolation between the Lurianically interpreted Kabbalistical tryptich (*Zimzum, Shevirath Hakelim, Tikkun*) and their apparently coincidental architectural counterparts (*construction,* (de)*construction,* (re)*construction*) can no longer be ignored.

The history of Western architecture is indelibly stained by an obstinate optimism traced solely by constructive attitudes signified by construction. (in)*Formed* by anthropocentrism, architects have obligated themselves mimetically to repeat the paradisic (un)*equal* hierarchical relationship by subordinating self to that first perfect architect – God – by whose hand man's initial, and only ideal, home – the Garden of Eden – was conceived. Traditionally, the overwhelming desire to 'get it right' has been (re)*presented* by buildings suppressing any trace of a 'wound' (or, for that matter, (re)*pressing* the passage of time – and with it – suppressing the only hope of healing that wound). The sign of intrinsic optimism was manifest in construction, ie, that belief in being, or existence, that the Bible (later [re]*written* by

Heidegger) addresses.

Whatever the nature of construction – its style, its context, its bias – the implicit optimism of the human spirit innocently, if (in)*advertently,* suppressed 'mistakes' so as to mimetically express mankind's (un)*equal,* and (im)*perfect,* relationship to a divine being. Equal to Luria's Kabbalistical interpretation of 'Zimzum' (God's withdrawal, making way for mankind), anthropocentrism, ie, the inference of mankind's assuming 'centre stage', to better act out this primary (in)*equality,* was effected. Edenically, Zimzum can be interpreted as God's establishing of authority by the Genesis divine denial ('do not eat of the tree in the centre of the garden') which (through God's withdrawal), leaves 'centre stage' available for Adam and Eve to either obey, or to overturn, that mandate. Either way, Adam and Eve are given a primary message by God (un)*alterably* demanding a response. God's withdrawal makes Adam's and Eve's presence possible. By responding at all (never mind which response), Adam and Eve establish their own presence, which in turn, signifies God's absence – or – His withdrawal.

Similarly, the establishing of a corresponding architecture – one that responds mimetically to that first, perfect place made by the hand of God (Eden) – not only commits architecture to a perpetually (im)*perfect* condition, but ironically (re)*moves* the trace of that (im)*perfection* as it suppresses any possibility of erring in favour of 'getting it right'. The very nature of architecture since that time is couched in the (pre)*tension* of the architect trying to get it right by reducing the passage of time to a condition of absence – conscious removal.

As an architectural analogue to Zimzum and as an epilogue to the passion play of Christianity, the architect assumes a position of presence – a kind of divine (re)*placement* - so as to 'create' mimetically derived iterations of an imagined innocent state equated with perfection. For almost 2,000 years architects have denied the 'trace' of that perpetual wound which nostalgically draws mankind back to an originally innocent state. (im)*Possible* to attain, (il)*logical* to conceive, architects nonetheless persistently strive to reduce the distance between the problems of mimesis as they attempt to concretise divine ideals into a never-to-be-achieved state of innocence.

God's withdrawal allows mankind to (dis)*place* Him, and by their own (re)*placement,* they attempt to accomplish similar goals. With the coming of Christianity, faith or belief in an ideal (re)*enforces* architects' resolve as they attempt to (re)*place* a heavenly garden inhabited by 'named' creatures with a mimetically conceived divine city resurrecting mankind from the original fall from grace. While Christian faith is the final, synthesising element in Hegel's tripartite philosophical project (first Greek, then Jew and, finally, Christian), it becomes the first in a new tripartite series (Zimzum), followed by the apocolyptical view of the world metaphorised by the breaking of the vessels (Shevirath Hakelim), and concluded by continuously failed attempts to heal an irreparable wound (Tikkun).

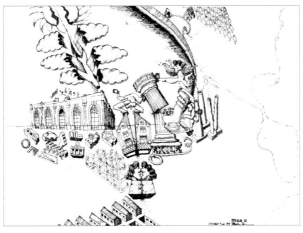

STANLEY TIGERMAN, *EXILE II, CHICAGO TO LA,* 1984

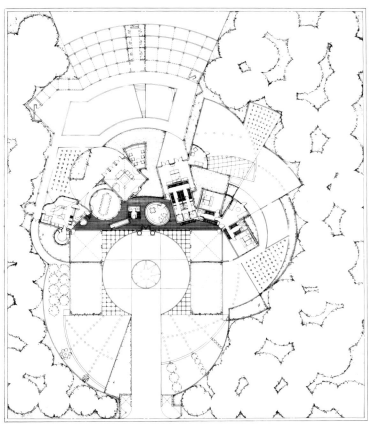

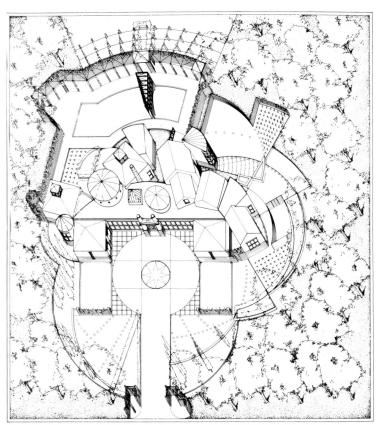

STANLEY TIGERMAN, PRIVATE RESIDENCE, HIGHLAND PARK, ILLINOIS, 1988-90, *ABOVE L TO R*: SITE PLAN; AXONOMETRIC; *BELOW FROM TOP*: REAR AND FRONT ELEVATIONS; SECTION

ABOVE L TO R: EXTERIOR, DETAILS:

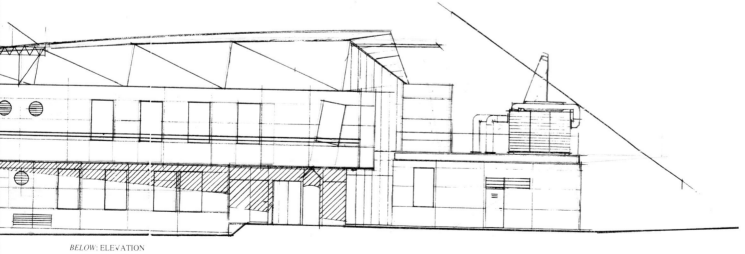

BELOW: ELEVATION

INTERIOR VIEW OF CONCEPTUAL ORRERY

EXTERIOR VIEW

Kate Mantilini, Restaurant; Santa Monica

INTERIOR DETAIL SHOWING FLOORING

This project was to convert an existing 6,400 square feet commercial bank into a 24-hour restaurant: 'A roadside steakhouse for the future, with a clock' (Marilyn Lewis).

Set on the northwest corner of a major urban intersection attached to a parking structure in a mid-rise office complex in Beverly Hills, California, a new building (wall) is entrapped in the old (column).

Building, fresco and sculpture, which are simultaneously discrete and associated, unite within a single framework. The poche wall of the new building engulfs the columns of the old. The wall is constructed of a four-person increment. The building is conceived as a permanent work.

A roof-scape of walls, mechanical-equipment rooms and sun dial are at the service of the adjacent tower workers.

A conceptual orrery, piercing through a 14 feet diameter occulus, summarises the reflective or interpretative intentions of the project. This mechanism – made of the building (distilling and condensing the essential aesthetic fabric) – is in the process of making or describing the building. The prickly cactus-like exterior, vacillating between surface and volume, maintains a tactile sensibility.

(This project requires a 'reading' in terms other than those of sight alone.) A psychological profile of this building reveals aggressive, obsessive, active characteristics, though tempered by a coolness and somewhat business-like politeness.

The interior space is vaguely exterior. Its hall-like quality reflects its public intention. People within this space tend to be extremely conscious of their position.

AXONOMETRIC

ABOVE: VIEW OF RESTAURANT FROM ENTRANCE; *BELOW*: INTERSECTION OF NEW BUILDING WITH OLD

INTERIOR VIEW OF HALL